Filmmaking for Beginners

FILMMAKING
FOR BEGINNERS

by Joan Horvath

THOMAS NELSON INC., PUBLISHERS
Nashville, Tenn. • New York, New York

he Collegiate School for Boys, New York City

First edition

Library of Congress Cataloging in Publication Data

Horvath, Joan.
   Filmmaking for beginners.

   SUMMARY: Discusses equipment, terminology, and techniques for
amateur film makers.
   1. Cinematography—Juvenile literature.
[1. Cinematography]   I. Title.
TR851.H657   778.5'3   74-701
ISBN 0-8407-6375-1

Contents

CHAPTER 1

Movies by Amateurs

Walt Whitman said that "To have great poets, there must be great audiences, too." If such is the case, then in the not-too-distant future we should be having great film makers as well as great filmgoers. New audiences for the art of film are being created every day in schools, community workshops, colleges, and universities—even in the home basement.

Neighborhood film groups are organizing everywhere. Children, from the primary grades up, are learning how to create films both for their own pleasure and to express what they feel and want to communicate to others. All over the country, children and teachers are attending workshops where they learn the basic techniques of filmmaking. They then take their acquired skills back to the classroom and turn out delightful, innovative projects. Films by children have already been shown on network television and are being distributed to schools across the country. It is reasonable to say that film is often the language of today's child. We have been in the midst of a communications revolution in this country for a number of years. The result has been a new kind of student, with new horizons, a new language, and new tools for the expression of that language.

It was probably in the middle of the 1960's that film production by youngsters began to take on a serious impetus. The Eastman Kodak Company gave a boost to the movement in 1967 when it introduced the new Super 8 film format. This new film gauge and the technical equipment for its use made relatively inexpensive equipment available to teachers, who

The Collegiate School for Boys, New York City

began to recognize film as the contemporary medium. The 8mm and Super 8 film was not only cheaper than the 16mm and 35mm gauge, but it was also cartridge-loading, which made it much easier for small children to handle.

New cameras came out in the 1960's. They had automatic exposure meters and electric eyes. They were easier to carry. The chance of making a mistake was greatly lessened. Late in the Sixties, the American Film Institute was founded, as were other national organizations concerned with film and education. Soon film clubs and societies were springing up in schools.

Film production today occurs at all levels. Over twenty-five colleges and universities in the United States offer academic programs of film study leading up to a Ph.D. Another two

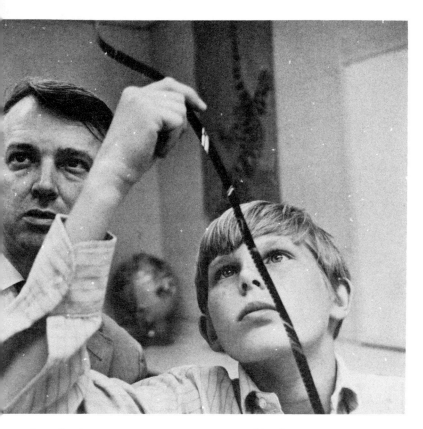

hundred institutions give courses in film history, appreciation, criticism, or production, and at least one hundred operate their own professional film units.

Where once the only interest in filmmaking was as a passive entertainment, there is now very active involvement—and a constantly growing amount of it. Five-year-old children are making movies. They are learning how to make their own slides and viewers, how to make a camera from a shoe box, and even how to animate their own simple drawings. They edit, direct, operate cameras, act, write scripts, and create sound tracks for both 8 and 16mm films.

Each year many film contests are held. Perhaps the oldest and best known are the annual Kodak Movie Awards. Each year Kodak offers as its grand prize a six-week cinema-study scholarship at the college level, which includes work in a Hollywood studio. This contest began in 1962, and presently its five categories are open to all young film makers through the age of nineteen. The awards are sponsored by the Eastman Kodak Company in cooperation with the University Film Foundation and CINE (The Council on International Non-Theatrical Events). There is no limit to the subjects the individual film maker can choose to enter. More information about this annual contest can be obtained from:

> Teenage Movie Awards
> Eastman Kodak Company
> Department 840
> Rochester, New York 14650

We don't have to look far to cite examples of young people's activity in filmmaking. Children in Kansas City, Missouri, presented their own comment on the impact of television upon current society. With great insight and humor they produced, in conjunction with a local art gallery, a delightful animated film called *Gone With the Antennas*. The Saint Francis School in Goshen, Kentucky, has made film study and filmmaking an integral part of their school curriculum. In Dayton, Ohio, three second-grade boys at the Jefferson Primary School pooled their talents to create *The Treasure Hunt*, a five-minute adventure film. A class of children in Washington, D.C., created their own version of the English epic *Beowulf* and also concocted a pie-throwing slapstick comedy.

Four- and five-year-olds at New York's Bank Street School of Education have taken their cameras out on the street and filmed their view of their own neighborhood. *Three Space Mice*, an animated film about a trip that three mice take to the moon, was made by a group of six-, seven-, and eight-year-olds at the Agnes Russell School of Columbia University Teachers College.

Third graders in Oakland, California, have made several

successful animated films using clay figures and the stop-motion technique. Seventh graders in Toledo, Ohio, cooperated with the Toledo Museum of Art to produce a fantasy film about a young boy's journey through an art museum on a magic chair. The fifth-grade class at the East Falmouth Elementary School in Massachusetts constantly make animated films as independent projects. When this same group made their very first film, they used dots instead of pictures because they felt that they could not draw figures well enough.

In New York City there are many film projects under way by children in community centers, museums, schools, and workshops. One of the most active groups is the Children's Art Carnival in Harlem, where youngsters make short animated films that are shown to the accompaniment of taped music tracks. Manhattan's Collegiate School has a very active

The Collegiate School for Boys, New York City

filmmaking program, as does P.S. 138 in Brooklyn. Ten- to twelve-year-olds at the latter made a memorable three-and-a-half-minute indictment of a decaying community on one block and called it *Our Town.* A young girl used the Brooklyn Botanic Garden as the background for her lovely film *House of Color.*

There are now many organizations for the creation, study, and promotion of films by children. Young film makers can go to the Barnsdall Junior Arts Center in Los Angeles, California, for a "Super 8 Summer," a vacation-time training program. The Smithsonian Institution in Washington, D.C., has organized a children's film program. In 1970 the White House Conference on Children devoted several of its programs to films that had been made exclusively by youngsters.

Perhaps one of the most famous, most innovative, and most active of all the children's film workshops is the Yellow Ball Workshop in Lexington, Massachusetts. The director of the workshop, Yvonne Anderson, began her first experiments in film animation with children in 1963. Presently the workshop makes, rents, and sells films by children as young as five years old. All of them are 16mm sound films in color. At Ms. Anderson's workshop, youngsters learn techniques that include cutout animation, clay animation, tear-outs, drawing on film, papier-mâché animation, and animation with cells. Their creations have won prizes both in national and international festivals.

The Center for Understanding Media, Inc., in New York City is conducting model programs in filmmaking for elementary school children throughout the country. The Center began this endeavor by having teachers from Alaska, Nebraska, and Arkansas study film techniques at its headquarters during the summer. Also, film-makers-in-residence were sent to work with these teachers during the school year. This Artists-in-the-Schools Program gave each site a live-action film maker for three months and an animated film maker for another three months. They assisted in student productions and also screened, discussed, and analyzed films that had already been made. This was the first national film project to focus on the elementary schools, and it has now been expanded to include twenty-four states and the Virgin Islands.

The Center for Understanding Media also has a Young Directors' Center, which was organized to circulate for rent and sale exceptional films made by young people. The profits are used to help other youngsters in their film projects and experiments. To investigate this opportunity further, write to:

> Young Directors' Center
> Center for Understanding Media, Inc.
> 267 West 25th Street
> New York, New York 10001

The catalogue from this Center will give you an excellent idea of the range of topics.

Mark Adler is an example of the ingenuity and imagination of the young film maker today. When he was sixteen, he made *Good Day Sunshine* for only forty dollars. His film is now in the permanent archives of the Museum of Modern Art in New York City. Tod Gangler was fifteen and Rufus Seder was sixteen when they combined their talents to make *Very Grim Fairy Tales,* a three-minute work in which they managed to parody half a dozen well-known fairy tales. Cal Lewen has been making films since he was ten. He says he was drawn to the medium because "it is the perfect blend of art, intellect, and tinkering."

When Doug Smith was thirteen, he shot an 8mm film, eight minutes in length, which won a grand prize in the High School Film Festival.

Gross Gems is not a person's name, but the name of a film-production company made up entirely of teen-age moguls. They have made more than six films and specialize in entertainment, humor, and "special effects."

There is no question that interest in film among children is widespread and at an all-time high. Many educators have now begun to refer to the child's appreciation of film as his "visual literacy." There is no escaping the fact that we are today a media-centered world, and film is part of our contemporary language. Learning to appreciate films, learning to

The Collegiate School for Boys, New York City

make films can help the child in expressing himself, in developing his tastes and critical powers. It can train him to see with a perceptive eye. Making films can introduce the youngster to new experiences that are pleasing and enriching. His social growth can also be enhanced as he learns how to work in production units with others. Learning the basic skills of filmmaking and applying them in personal, creative experiments can be, if nothing else, a very special kind of fun.

CHAPTER 2

Motion Pictures and Motion-Picture Film

What is the difference between a still photograph and a "movie"? Probably the first answer that comes to mind is that a photograph is *still* while a movie *moves*. Although this difference might seem like a basic description of the two, it is not really accurate. The truth is that motion pictures do not really move at all. They only appear to move. "But I have seen movies," you might reply, "and they certainly looked to me as if they were moving." You are right, of course. But when you watch a movie, what you are actually seeing is a series of still photographs rapidly shot and rapidly projected in succession. When you shoot a film, you are really shooting a rapid-fire series of still photographs—one on each frame of film.

The "motion" of motion pictures is, in reality, a trick of the eye, an optical illusion. Many experts tell us that optical illusions are tricks of the mind as well as of the eye. To prove that movies are really a series of still pictures, take a look at the illustration of exposed motion-picture film, a strip of 35mm gauge. You can readily see that each frame is a single photograph. However, when the film is put in a projector and run through at the proper speed, movement is created— that is, the illusion of movement.

Even if you have no projector, no camera, and no film stock, you can still prove this point in a very simple way. Take a small memo pad, or about twenty-five small index cards,

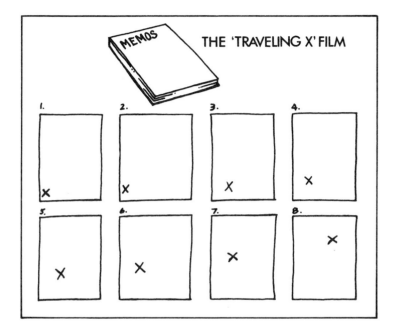

or twenty-five pieces of paper of equal size. In your mind let each page correspond to a single frame of film. On each "frame," or page, make a small x, as in the illustrated example. On the first page make an x in the lower left corner of the frame. On the second page make an x of the same size slightly higher and very slightly to the right of where you placed the one on the first page. Repeat the procedure on each of the successive pages, always making the x slightly higher and slightly to the right of the one preceding it. Your last x on the last frame or page should be in the upper right-hand corner.

Now, quickly flip the pages in rapid succession, and you will find that you have created a little movie about a traveling x. The symbol will seem to move across the "screen" from left to right. If you like, you can attempt to create a variety of movement. Instead of gliding across the screen, your x will wriggle or dance if you just tilt its position slightly, right and then left, one movement to a page.

When you draw your x on each page you are doing the same thing that happens, technically, inside your camera during the process of shooting a film. The flipping of the memo pages or index cards compares to the projection of that same piece of film.

In talking about movies or motion, you must consider both the speed of taking the film and the speed of projecting it. That is important for you to know, for you will not want to capture action at normal speed every time you shoot. Sometimes you will want to vary that speed in order to create

The Collegiate School for Boys, New York City

special effects—a friend running through a field in "slow motion," or maybe your mother cleaning her entire house in three minutes flat as a result of "speeded-up action." Learn the rules now. Then, if you choose, you will be able to successfully break them later. After learning the principles of the medium, you can adapt them to anything you want to do.

Your "movie" camera, then, takes a series of still photographs at so many frames (or still photos) a second, and these photos are projected at so many frames (or still photos) a second. You probably have seen many features in movie houses in your neighborhood. The projectors in these theaters project the frames of the film at 24 frames a second. Most experts agree that this is the speed at which the illusion will have the realistic, natural movement of life itself—or life as we seem to see it with our naked eye. What this means (and you might try out this statistic on your friends) is that when you go to a theater and watch a feature film, which usually runs about ninety minutes, you are actually looking at almost 130,000 single photographs or frames!

This projection speed of 24 frames a second is sound projection speed. Before sound came to film, however, the projection speed was 16 frames per second. Part of this difference was due to the fact that the early projectors were not automatic, so the projectionist had to crank them by hand. Speeds varied with the strength of the projectionist's arm. But once sound and the automatic projectors came in, the 24-frames-per-second figure was set and human error was removed.

FOOTAGE SPEEDS AT WHICH STOCKS RUN THROUGH A PROJECTOR

35mm	90 feet per minute
16mm	36 feet per minute
Super 8mm	14.8 feet per minute
8mm	13.5 feet per minute

Super 8 and 8mm are the gauges you will most likely be

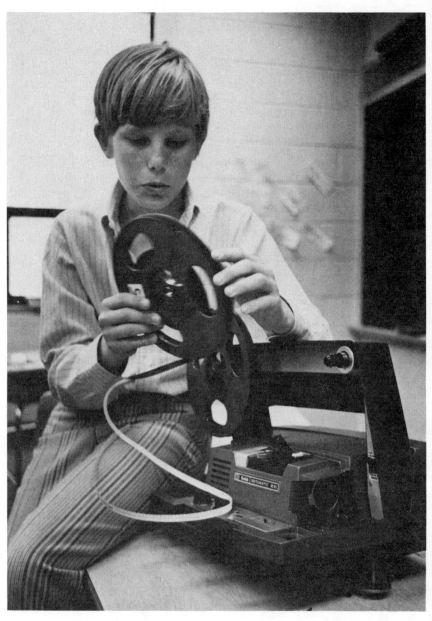

The Collegiate School for Boys, New York City

working with—at least in the beginning. In these two gauges the shooting rate and the rate of projection for the illusion of natural-looking action is not the customary 24 frames per second. Rather, it is 18 frames per second, because most films in these gauges are silent films, and 24 frames per second is the projection rate for sound film. A good Super 8 sound projector will have provisions for showing a sound

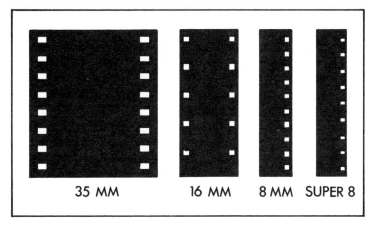

35 MM   16 MM   8 MM   SUPER 8

Film gauges

film at the rate of 24 frames per second as well as silent film at 18 frames per second.

The word *gauges* has been mentioned several times. Perhaps you are wondering just what is meant by that expression. Let's go back to our local neighborhood movie house. When you see a film there, the chances are that it has been shot in 35mm gauge. This means the film frame is 35 millimeters wide. The screen on which these frames are projected can be up to sixty feet wide. Many spectaculars in recent years have been shot in 70mm, which is twice as large as 35mm stock (stock is the film itself). Sometimes, though,

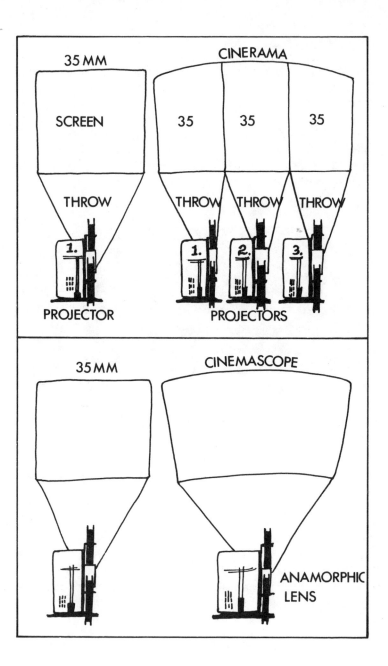

these films are not shot in 70mm, but are blown up to that gauge in a special laboratory through a process called "wet-gate." There is a larger area in the margin of 70mm film stock, and this enables the film maker to use stereophonic sound because there is room for another track. When you put several sound tracks on the same film stock, you can create an impressive effect in a theater, because the sound can come from several speakers scattered throughout the house.

In recent years there have been further variations on these formats. These were created to have an impressive and spectacular effect upon moviegoers. But like most special effects, they are not impressive unless the movie itself is.

Cinemascope uses the 35mm film stock, but the cameras are equipped with a special device called an anamorphic lens. This lens is able to squeeze an image horizontally to half its normal size, and thereby record a much wider view. When this film is projected in the movie house, another special lens on the projector unsqueezes the squeezed image, and what we see is twice as large as the normal 35mm film.

Some of us have been swept almost directly into the action and adventure of a film by the process known as Cinerama. In this process three cameras shoot the same scene, each using the regular 35mm stock. The difference is that each camera covers only a third of the scene or viewing angle. When a Cinerama film is projected, three projectors run simultaneously. If you have ever viewed a Cinerama production, you may have noticed a barely discernible seam —or slight separation—on the screen between each of the three parts.

The gauge that is the real workhorse of the entire film industry is the 16mm format. This began in home movies, but was soon adopted by government and industry for making training and educational films. TV news departments began to rely on it heavily. Then it became the stock of the serious but nonwealthy independent film maker, who would make feature films in 16mm and then blow them up to 35mm for projection in theaters. Probably more of this stock than any other is sold to film makers today. Most educational films shown in school classrooms are made and shown in 16mm. Many of the feature films (especially classics) have been reduced from 35mm to 16mm for showing in schools and to community groups. There are several dozen 16mm film festivals in this country each year.

The 8mm format, half as wide as the 16mm, replaced the latter in the workshops of home-movie fans. But now 8mm is itself rapidly being replaced by the relatively new Super 8. Although Super 8, like 8mm, is only eight millimeters wide, its frame image is half again as large. This is because the sprocket holes alongside the film are vertical instead of horizontal, thereby leaving a larger area for the picture itself. Generally speaking, the quality of color in Super 8 is greatly superior to 8mm. Super 8 is now being utilized with great success by very young film makers. With it, they can achieve the fine photography usually associated with the more "sophisticated" gauges.

If you are going to work in the 8mm or Super 8 format, you might like to know what kind of film is available to you. Although there are several film manufacturers, the raw stock of two of them offers all the various possibilities with which you might want to deal.

For 8mm motion-picture cameras, Eastman Kodak offers Kodachrome II film, which you can buy either in rolls or in metal magazines. Both roll and magazine contain fifty feet of film stock. You can purchase this Kodachrome II film in "Daylight" or in "Type A." "A" stands for "artificial light," so Kodachrome II 8 mm Type A is usually used indoors with movie lights.

If you have a Super 8 camera, you can use Super 8 cartridges—the form in which most Super 8 film is packaged.

Also available in Super 8 are Kodachrome II Type A and Kodak Ektachrome 40 Type A. Both can be used indoors and outdoors.

Kodak has also developed a new high-speed color film available in Super 8 cartridges: Kodak Ektachrome 160 Type A. This film makes it possible for you to take your movies using only "available" or existing light—that is, no artificial lights, just the light that happens to be on the scene at the time you are filming. This is a definite plus. Kodak Ektachrome 160 is four times as fast as Kodak Ektachrome 40, so it can register the image much quicker and with much less light. Note, however, that if you want to use this special fast film, you must use with it a camera that can properly expose such a high-speed film. If you have any doubt about whether or not your camera can take this film, contact your camera manufacturer or distributor.

For black-and-white films instead of color, Kodak offers a choice of two stocks. The Kodak Plus-X Reversal Film 7276 is for general use. The Kodak Tri-X Reversal Film 7278, the high-speed counterpart of the Ektachrome 160, is ideal for scenes that are dimly lit.

Another source for film is Fujipan or Fujichrome Film. If you are working in the Fujica Single 8 System, your Fujica camera will accommodate *only* the Fujica Single 8 cartridge. Since Fujica cameras offer much versatility, having to use exclusively Fujica film is not a major drawback. The four stocks available include color for indoors, color for outdoors, medium-speed black and white, and high-speed black and white. One advantage of the Fujica cartridge is that you can wind the film backward in the Fujica camera, thereby creating your own in-camera trick effects such as dissolves and superimpositions.

Chances are, however, that most film you buy will be made by Kodak. But remember that Kodak itself does not process

The Collegiate School for Boys, New York City

black-and-white movie film, so ask your film dealer to suggest a laboratory that will develop it. If he cannot do so, write to Kodak:

> Eastman Kodak Company
> Department 841
> 343 State Street
> Rochester, New York 14650

CHAPTER 3

The Camera and Its Parts

Before you decide what kind of camera you would like, you should know what a camera does and how it does it.

To put it simply, a camera takes a picture. In the case of a motion-picture camera, it takes a series of photographs in rapid-fire succession. Motion-picture cameras have:

1. a viewing system for looking at the subject
2. a lens with various lens openings
3. a shutter that regulates the amount of light on the film
4. a motor for advancing the film
5. a receptacle to hold the film

Basically, there are two kinds of viewing systems. In the least expensive cameras, when you look through the eyepiece you are looking through a viewing lens that is not the same as the "taking" lens, or the lens that actually takes the picture. In other words, the viewfinder and the camera lens are two separate things, which means that the view you see is not *exactly* the one that the camera is taking. This divergence in views, referred to as "parallax," means there is about a one- or two-inch difference between your view and the camera's (see Illustration A). Parallax becomes a problem most often when you are moving in for tight, critical close-ups. You can compensate for it somewhat by tipping the camera slightly in the direction of the viewfinder.

On the other hand, the single-lens reflex camera permits

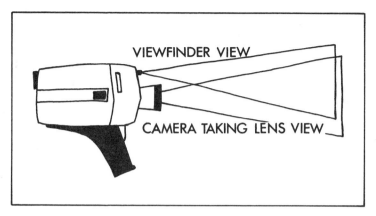

Illustration A

Illustration B

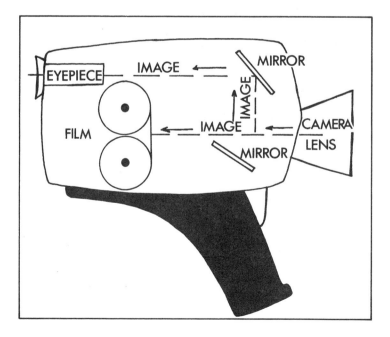

you to see through the viewfinder exactly what the camera lens is seeing and taking. Built-in mirroring devices pick up the image moving through the camera lens and transmit it, without variation, to your eyepiece viewer (see Illustration B).

A single-lens reflex system gives much more versatility to your camera because you know that the film is always registering exactly what you are seeing. This means you can more easily use a variety of filters and lenses.

You will most likely be using either of two general types of lens at first. The most elementary 8mm cameras are what we call "fixed-focus" cameras—that is, they are focused and permanently set at the factory. They will give you a sharp

When we focus on a nearby object, the *depth of field* is narrow and, basically, the background is out of focus.

When we focus on a distant object, the *depth of field* is greater. Both object and background are in focus.

image providing you are no closer than four feet to your subject. Lighting conditions also influence the effectiveness of the fixed-focus lens. For example, if the day is cloudy, you will probably not be able to get any closer to your subject than eight feet. In any case, if you have a fixed-focus camera, check your camera manual for the appropriate shooting distances.

Of course, the cameras with lenses that you focus yourself give you much more range and versatility. For sharp, clear pictures, it is important that you focus the lens at the proper distance setting. With a camera that is not fixed-focus, you must change the focus setting every time you change the distance between the camera and the subject.

Focusing such a camera is relatively simple. Mainly you should practice "seeing" through your eyepiece until you have trained your eye to adjust the lens to the point where the image is unmistakably sharp or in focus. Even then, do not be discouraged when you see your developed film. You will probably have to make several mistakes—thinking something is in focus when it is not—before you master focusing.

An important consideration here is the "depth of field," which is the amount of distance between the nearest and farthest objects that appear in acceptably sharp focus in your shot. When you focus on a nearby object, your depth of field is reduced. It is also reduced when lighting conditions are dim, or when you are using a telephoto lens or a zoom lens in the telephoto position.

Conversely, you increase the depth of field when you focus on distant objects, or when you use a small lens opening because of bright light, or when you use a wide-angle lens.

Most 8mm cameras have spring-driven motors for advancing the film, and it is wise to remember, if you have such a camera, to wind the motor after you have *completed* each shot. In this way you will automatically be prepared for the next one and will not wind down too soon. Nowadays, Super 8 cameras have battery-powered motors that make filmmaking more convenient by eliminating the necessity for winding. The batteries used in these cameras are generally of the alkaline type to ensure greater durability. Many cameras have indicators that tell when batteries are low in power.

Most professional cameras use electric motors. There are several kinds, depending on your needs. If you are shooting silent footage, you will want a motor whose speeds you can vary in order to make such shots as might require, say, slow motion or speeded-up motion. If you are shooting sound simultaneously with your visuals, you will need a "sync" sound camera with a "sync" sound motor, which can run constantly at 24 frames a second (the sound speed discussed earlier). These cameras can be portable (with the motor's power provided by batteries) or they can be plugged into AC outlets.

Many Super 8 cameras have the ability to run at variable speeds, making it possible to take slowed-down or accelerated action. In order to create a slow-motion effect, you must be able to "speed up" your camera—that is, the motor must advance the film faster than the regular 24 or 18 frames per second. For quite obvious slow motion, you should be able to advance your film speed to at least 48 frames per second. Conversely, in order to create the illusion of very fast action (à la a Keystone slapstick comedy), you must slow down the speed at which your film advances to at least 12 frames per second.

For slow motion: Speed up advancing film
For speeded-up action: Slow down advancing film

Many cameras also have what is called a "single-framing" capability. This means that your camera is able to take one frame of film (that is, a single photograph) at a time. This capability is very important if you want to create your own animation. For example, place a friend of yours at one end of a city block, and place your camera in the center of that block (keeping the camera perfectly still and secure on a tripod). Then shoot only one frame at a time, having your friend move a few inches forward between each frame or picture. When this segment of film is projected at regular speed, it will seem as if your friend is gliding magically up the block. But remember, move only the actor, never the camera!

Controlling the exposure of your film is another difficult matter—even though most Super 8 cameras now have either automatic exposure controls or a built-in electronic device that lets you know when there is sufficient light on your subject for proper exposure. If the automatic exposure control on your camera has a film-speed dial, just set it for the speed of the film that you are using. This means setting it for the film's "ASA" rating, which is printed on the film package and in the informational material accompanying your film.

To control exposure, you must use the proper lens opening on your camera. If the exposure control on your camera must be adjusted manually, just set your lens opening according to the exposure table that appears on your film stock instruction sheet. You must set the lens opening according to the lighting condition of the scene you are going to photograph: the more light is needed, the larger your lens opening will have to be.

Lens openings are measured in "F stops," and stop numbers range from F 1.4 to F 22. The F stop measures the amount of light passed by the lens at different exposure settings. F 1.4 would let in the most light; F 22 would let in the least amount. Remember, the lower the F stop number, the greater the amount of light that enters. The higher the F stop number, the less the amount of light. This is important to know, not only for getting the proper amount of light on your subject, but also for creating any number of different effects. Deliberately overexposing a subject by letting more light in than is necessary can create an eerie effect. You can create silhouettes by underexposing your main subject and exposing for the brightest element around it. On pages 38–39 is a series of three photographs taken of the same person in the same setting. Each shot, however, was taken at a different lens opening to create a different effect.

Kodak offers the following as a standard daylight exposure table for average front-lighted subjects. These are the minimal ranges on most inexpensive cameras:

F 16	For bright or hazy sun
	On light sand or snow
F 11	For bright or hazy sun where there are distinct shadows
F 8	For cloudy or bright sun where there are no shadows
F 5.6	For heavy overcast
	For open shade

There are both normal and special lenses for cameras, and they are determined by their focal length. For 35mm cameras the focal length of the normal lens is 50 millimeters. The 25mm lens is considered normal for 16mm, and the 13mm lens is rated normal for 8mm. But special lenses have been developed that can create almost any effect desired. Three of them are the telephoto lens, the wide-angle lens, and the zoom lens. Put simply, the wide-angle lens allows you to photograph a greater area than the normal lens while still remaining close to the subject. The telephoto lens lets you photograph a smaller area of the scene at a greater distance from it. A zoom lens allows you to move in close to a subject or pull away from it while you are filming.

The telephoto lens magnifies the image, and since whenever an image is magnified, the camera motion too is magnified, it is recommended that telephoto lenses be used with

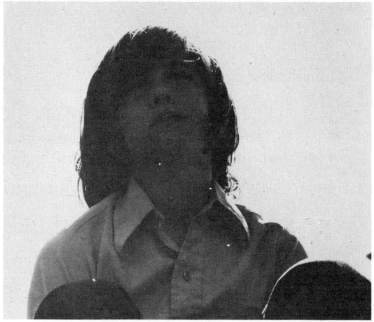

The same subject, but for each shot the "F" stop was changed, creating a different effect. Gradually, the light was closed down on the subject until a silhouette was achieved.

a secure tripod. Also, since the telephoto lens creates a very shallow depth of field, you will have to change your focus during the shot to keep your subject in the focal field. Most sophisticated Super 8 cameras change focus automatically with their telephoto lenses.

With a telephoto lens you can shoot, from a distance, a subject that you would have to shoot at close range with a normal lens. That means you can photograph action that you might not be able to get close to readily. You can also

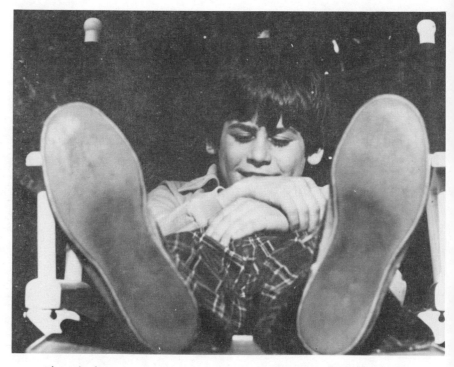

The telephoto lens can be used to distort the action. The boy's shoes seem to be as large as his body; the baseball bat looks gigantic.

Photos by Stemm

select what you wish to be in focus in the shot—to create special effects. The background behind a human subject can almost be made to disappear with the telephoto lens, achieving a more abstract and three-dimensional effect. Using the same person, you can take him out of focus and bring the background into focus. A telephoto lens can radically alter our perspective on the action taking place on film. For example, a girl holding a bouquet of flowers by her side will appear to be in normal perspective, but when she puts that bouquet in front of her, it will look much larger in proportion. Say you want to shoot a group of automobiles coming at you. If you use a telephoto lens set several hundred feet away from them, they would appear not to be moving very rapidly at all; they would also appear to be in the same plane of action. You might have seen this effect on TV, where it is

frequently used to show a pretty girl running toward the camera in a field (usually in slow motion), and she seems to be almost running in place. The telephoto lens can create some interesting effects because of its ability to flatten out action to a very narrow plane.

The wide-angle lens has a much greater depth of field than the normal lens or the telephoto lens, and it is for this reason that it is mainly used. It lets you get very close to your subject and still lets you have a wide view, and it can achieve angles and distortions that are impossible with other lenses.

The telephoto lens has the effect of putting all the subjects into the same place, although they are actually at a distance from each other. Both boys appear to be at the net.

The wide-angle lens lets you get close to your subject and still have a wide view. You can achieve distortions and angles that are difficult with regular lenses.

Photo by Stemm

Since you are shooting in close, it exaggerates motion, and its effect on action leaving or coming toward the lens is exactly the opposite of that of the telephoto. If you want to film your friends in a fistfight (acted, of course), try using a

The Eclair 16 mm. NPR

Courtesy of The Eclair Corporation of America

wide-angle lens. You will be able to cover most of the action. And if you move close, the fists and punches thrown will be greatly distorted in the frame.

The zoom lens is really a variable focal-length lens. You are probably very familiar with this lens by now. Just remember that it should be used sparingly if it is going to be effective. Audiences can become very annoyed with the beginning film maker's tendency to zoom in and out of everything he sees in his camera's path.

For theatrical shooting in 35mm, the Mitchell BNC camera is usually used for "sync"-sound shooting. For silent shooting in 35mm, the Arriflex 35 is widely used. There are many 16mm cameras available. Perhaps the most popular are the Arriflex BL, the Auricon Cine-Voice, and the Eclair NPR (see page 44) for "sync"-sound filming. The Eclair, by the way, is now very widely used because it is comparatively lightweight and thus easily portable. This camera is able to take loads of at least 400 feet in its magazine (the container attached to the

Kodak Instamatics M22, M24, M26, M28, M30
Courtesy of Eastman Kodak Company

camera that houses the film stock). For silent 16mm shooting, there are the Arriflex S model, the Eclair, the Bolex Reflex 16, and the Beaulieu Reflex.

The 8mm and Super 8 cameras, which are the ones you will most likely be using, are becoming increasingly sophisticated. There are several, so you will have a choice when you consider purchasing one. Kodak puts out a series of instamatic movie cameras that are very inexpensive. The lowest-priced camera has a fixed-focus lens and, like the rest, is cartridge-loading. Recently, Kodak made available the Kodak XL33, which accommodates the very high-speed Ektachrome 160 film (Type A). With this relatively easy-to-operate camera, you can photograph in very dim light. You can even take color movies of outdoor scenes at night. This camera has a built-in electric exposure control.

Another relatively inexpensive camera that accepts the new

The Kodak XL33 Super 8

Courtesy of Eastman Kodak Company

The Canon Auto Zoom 318M

Courtesy Canon Inc. Japan

ASA 160 film is the Canon Auto Zoom 318M. This camera has a bright F 1.8 lens, power zooming, and a capability for shooting very tight close-ups.

The Yashica Electro 8LD-6 allows you to make in-camera dissolves, fade-ins, and fade-outs. It has through-the-lens reflex viewing, and the lens itself is a very fast F 1.8. It can focus from infinity down to as close as one meter, and its filming speeds include 18, 24, and 36 frames per second. It also has a single-framing capability.

The Bell and Howell Focus-Matic 672/XL camera has an F 1.3 lens, and is also capable of taking the new ASA 160 film. It has a 24mm zoom lens and reflex viewing, and the Focus-matic system makes sharp focusing almost inevitable.

Its automatic exposure control, power or manual zoom, and externally viewed footage counter make it a fine mid-range-priced camera (about $200).

Bolex offers several cameras. Perhaps the one with the most capabilities is the Bolex 280 Macrozoom. It has a two-speed power zoom and gives you the ability to shoot extreme close-ups as well as powerful telephoto shots. This camera is also capable of in-camera fade-ins and fade-outs.

The Nikon 8X Super Zoom has a behind-the-lens meter system and a 1-to-82 ratio for zooming. It is capable of three filming speeds and can do single framing.

Courtesy Bell & Howell

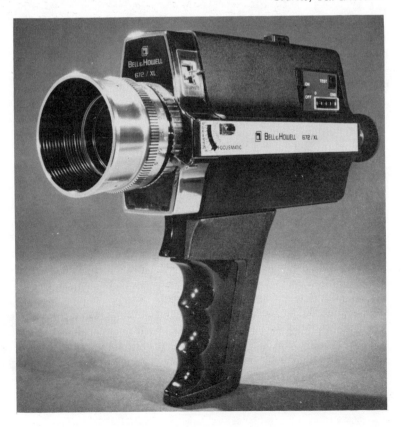

The Fujica Single-8 Z450

Courtesy Fuji Photo Film, U.S.A., Inc.

The Honeywell Elmo Super Filmatic 110
Courtesy Honeywell Elmo Photographic Products

The Fujica Single-8 Z450 features a precision zoom lens, an electric-eye exposure control, variable shutter speeds, through-the-lens viewing, and three film speeds. It is relatively simple to operate, but remember, it accepts only Fuji film.

One of the most versatile cameras to come along is the Honeywell Elmo Super Filmatic 110. It is also expensive ($500)—if economy is a factor in your camera buying. It has an extremely powerful zoom lens with which you can shoot between 7mm ultra-wide angle and 70mm super-telephoto. It has a power zoom that takes about eight seconds to complete. With this camera you can shoot single frame, regular speeds, or slow motion up to 54 frames a second (most cameras go up only to 36 frames a second). It has through-the-lens viewing and an automatic exposure system with manual override. It accepts all the film stock speeds, and has a built-in filter for outdoor filming. The camera also offers remote control for still more versatility.

CHAPTER 4

Expressing Yourself in Film

There is now nothing to stop you from taking your camera, loading it with film, and going out and shooting whatever pops into your mind, or whatever you see in front of you. This is an excellent way to learn to become facile with your camera. You can practice exposing properly, focusing sharply, framing, composition—in short, you can become very dexterous with your mechanical instrument. But that is practice. It is not a movie.

Just imagine what you might do if you were asked to compose a poem, write a novel or a short story, create an essay, or paint a picture. Given your choice of subjects and themes, you would first select the one that appealed to you the most. In executing it—in whatever medium you selected—you would draw on your personal knowledge and experiences. Even if you were creating a fantasy, you would begin with reality as you know it.

If you wanted your story or poem to be unique, you would try to put as much of yourself in it as you possibly could. Most likely, in fact, you would not be able to help expressing, in some way or other, your personal feelings toward the subject or theme. You would present the material from your own point of view—something that is singularly yours and no one else's. It is the same with motion pictures.

Nowadays we have come to refer to theatrical motion pictures as, say, a Fellini movie, an Ingmar Bergman film, or an Alfred Hitchcock picture. Many film critics now operate from the *auteur* theory of film criticism, which recognizes the dominant vision of one artist upon the entire work. Even though large productions require large staffs of technicians and artisans, all of them serve essentially the vision of a single person. The film is his statement, his poem, his novel, his portrait, his painting. Even the fledgling or mini-moviemaker requires assistance from others and, of course, must know how to use these assistants in the most effective way—but even he must be faithful to his own point of view.

Faithfulness to one's own vision—the way one feels about the subject one is dealing with and the emotional feelings that led to that choice in the first place—is basic to creative expression in any craft or art. Even simple home movies of your family or friends can be much more exciting if they have a point of view.

At this point, as you are getting your feet wet in filmmaking, it is good to decide what it is about yourself that draws you to this medium. Chances are you will have an audience for whatever film or films you make. It may include friends, teachers, parents, or even strangers. Perhaps in your movie you want not only to entertain them, but also to tell them how you feel about something important to you, and to try and get them to feel the same way. Let's suppose you are making a film—or want to make a film—about someone you love very much, such as your mother. As you begin to plan the film, you will try to find the best way to present her, the best way to create a portrait of her that will make her appealing to the audience.

Thinking about your point of view should help you to approach your material with a great sense of freedom. Make up your mind now that if you are going to make movies, you will never be afraid to experiment, never be afraid to make mistakes. The most elaborate motion picture in the world is created with a multitude of mistakes.

The main thing to remember in making films is that you are doing much more than taking pictures. The camera takes the pictures, but the eye and mind and heart behind it de-

Your point of view can change the way we see the city.

A rainy day, close-up and long shot. The point of view is realistic.
Photos by Stemm

cide what the pictures will be, how they will fit together, and what effect they will have on others. Two film makers, for example, can both make a film about a large city. One will shoot the city in such a way that it looks ugly, dirty, noisy, soulless. The other will take the same subject and, with his treatment, create a beautiful, haunting, sympathetic

A rainy day. Here the point of view deals with patterns, light, and shadow.

portrait of a large metropolis. The difference begins at the very beginning with each film maker's personal point of view.

To clarify "point of view," let's consider some subjects that you might choose for a film and see how you might express yourself in them.

People write essays and editorials constantly with the purpose of making the reader aware of a condition and getting him to take some kind of action about it. You might decide to create a film editorial, let us say, on the subject of pollution. As your point of view, you might elect to trace the life cycle of a pair of cans or bottles discarded by the roadside. Or, on a more extravagant level you might show through them what the people in your school or community are doing in the fight against pollution.

Portraits are painted, portraits are created in words, and portraits are produced in films. You may have decided that you want to create a cinematic portrait of your dog. But you want to do it in a way that is different from other movies about dogs and in a way that will be fun for an audience to watch. You hit upon a unique point of view. What if, after you showed your dog playing or eating or licking your sister's face, you showed what the world looked like from *his* vantage point? Therefore, you decide to shoot much of your film from the next-to-the-ground angle of your dog. We call this the *subjective* camera. Used sparingly, it can be revealing and effective. It lets us enter directly into the world of the subject itself.

You may also decide that you want your film to be a kind of poem, a simple, memorable study of something that we all come into contact with but seldom appreciate for its loveliness. So, when the other film makers are waiting for sunny days to shoot, you take your camera out on a rainy day and look for simple shots that will show people what they do not normally bother to look at: close-ups of droplets running down a window, reflections in a large puddle, raindrops making large circles in a stream, small rivulets coursing down an umbrella, drops falling on flowers.

By using what is now called time-lapse photography, someone once created an unusual cinematic poem about the birth and death of an ice cube. Subjects and materials for our cameras lie all around us!

How do you feel about eating? If you think eating is one of man's major passions, you might want to make your own humorous statement about it. You can take your camera to a fair, to a picnic, or to an outdoor barbecue, and catch a variety of shots of people engaged in chewing, biting, chomping, eating slowly, eating quickly, eating delicately, eating grossly. If you can also get a tape recorder and record the sounds of eating, you should wind up with a film that is both a comment and hilarious entertainment.

Many painters have painted still lifes—flowers in a vase, fruit in a bowl—and you can choose to do the same thing, but this time with the added advantage of motion. All you need is a common object—let us say a ball—and only one movie light. Keep the object and your camera steady, and move only the light. The result will be a fascinating study of light and shadow, and the shaping of the various forms that the ball will assume.

We have all read fairy tales. We have all read science-fiction fantasies. Suppose you decided to have a fantastic point of view in your film. The possibilities are as limitless as your imagination. Take a very common subject. For example, the supermarket. If you use the technique of speeded-up motion, the people in the supermarket will appear to be greedily pulling things off the shelves as fast as they can get them. What if you then decide to make up your own situation? Suppose some of the people suddenly had tails. If you have some friends who are willing to be your actors, who will help you make the "tails" and will wear them among strangers, you might be able to create a delightful film about how people spontaneously react to something

By moving a single light around a tennis ball, we can create a variety of effects.

radically different in their midst—and show how different life might be for the tail wearers. It is recommended that if you attempt something like this, you keep your camera as inconspicuous as possible, or the reactions you are looking for will not be genuine.

An excellent example of how a point of view creates a specific, personal film can be seen in the approach toward filming the zoo as a subject. If you want to show the zoo as a place of pleasure and fun—because that is what you believe it to be—you will choose to select happy visuals: children laughing at the animals, seals playing in the water and barking for food, monkeys swinging gaily from bar to bar, birds flitting on branches, lions and tigers comfortably asleep in the sun—in short, both people and animals enjoying themselves.

Our point of view is to show the player in graceful movement.

But suppose your point of view is different. Perhaps you disapprove of animals being caged up simply so people can look at them. Then, certainly, the visuals you would chose would be radically different. You might show children taunting the animals, or emphasize many bars and cages in your shots, or pick as many close-ups of sad-looking animal faces as you could possibly find. With the same subject, then, you would make a completely different film, a completely different statement—you would offer a completely different personal expression.

The same idea holds true for a subject that Hollywood has dealt with many times over the course of the years: the airport. Airports are awfully large places. Why make a film on one? What is it you want to say with your film? How do you see the airport—and how do you want your audience to see it? Again, first, before all else, you need a point of view. Perhaps you want to show the technology, the mechanical operation: airplanes, takeoffs, landings, control tower, passenger and freight delivery. Perhaps you want to show one family sending their youngest child off on his first trip. Maybe you want to use the airport only as a background for a very human and tender study on people saying hello and good-bye. The choice is yours, depending on the statement you want to make.

Finally, suppose you are a sports fan and want to make a film about a particular sport. The kind of film you make will again depend on your point of view. If you love to ski and know a lot about the techniques involved, you might make a how-to film, showing others the basic rudiments of the sport. Or if you feel strongly about the beauty of skiing, you could make a film that captures the speed and grace of the skier as well as the beauty of the snowy landscape. You might choose to shoot much of your film in slow motion and elect to use a great deal of back lighting to bring added luster to the visuals (see Chapter 6 for a discussion of that special kind of lighting).

Our point of view is to show the player in awkward, clumsy motion.

Perhaps you are very fond of roller skating and also have a great sense of humor. You may decide that your film on roller skating will be a slapstick comedy. You will shoot as many pratfalls as you can at the roller rink. You will shoot them at regular speed, in slow motion, and in fast motion. Then you may edit them to a well-known piece of music. It will be your special way of looking at things, and your audience will be delighted with your point of view.

The possibilities are endless, but by now that should be obvious. Whatever your approach to films, the most valid one—and always the most successful—is the idea that is truly your own, the one in your own language. Say what you have on your mind and in your heart. Almost anyone can learn the techniques of filmmaking, but the rules and tools are valueless without individual imagination. You are the one who will give your film its real life. Express yourself.

CHAPTER 5

The Script

The plan for your film will generally emerge from the subject that you have selected, your viewpoint on that subject, and the effect you want your film to have on your audience.

No matter how brief your movie is, it should be complete. It should have an introduction, a body, and a conclusion, with appropriate continuity that combines all the elements. No matter what kind of movie you make, you are usually telling a story. After you have decided the kind of story you are going to tell, you should first write out a plan that will show the best way to proceed. Let us call this plan the script.

If the idea of writing a script frightens you, just relax. A script can take many shapes and forms, and at this stage in your development as a film maker, a script can be very simple—nothing more than a guide on which to base your actual shooting.

First of all, it is a good idea to decide what the overall form or category for your film will be. Are you going to make a documentary, a drama or comedy, a fantasy, an educational film? What style will express your film best? Let us say you are an avid ballplayer and want to make a film about your baseball team. You can do it any number of ways, in a variety of different styles. The choice is up to you—it will

The Documentary:
Before the Mountain Was Moved
Courtesy Contemporary Films/McGraw-Hill

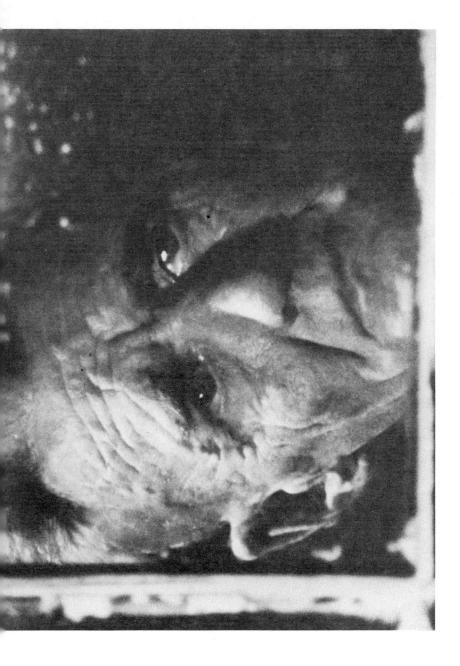

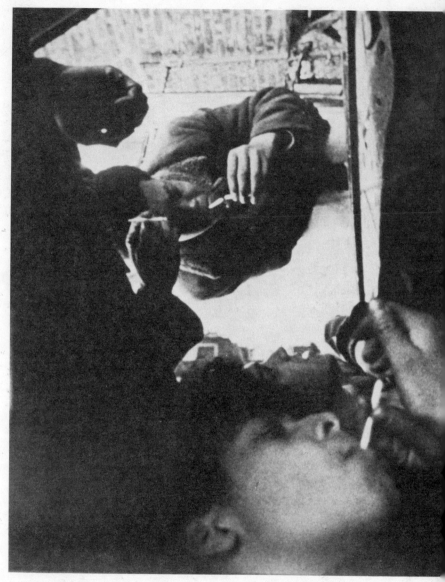

Not Me

The Drama:
Days and Nights in the Forest
Courtesy Contemporary Films/McGraw-Hill

be your point of view. You might want to show a typical game day: the players on your team, or on both teams, arriving for the game, practicing for it, playing it; the reactions of the fans who are watching; the joy of the winning team; the disappointment of the losing team. Your approach would then be essentially realistic. You would be shooting things as they happened. Thus you would be making a kind of news document of the game day—or a "documentary."

On the other hand, perhaps there are two members of your team who are generally in conflict with each other. You might decide to dramatize this conflict on film. One of the two team members has a great deal of personal difficulty in adjusting to team spirit and cooperation; he is mostly interested in his own personal accomplishments and glory. A situation can be set up in which he ultimately learns that only by playing together with the others can he avoid conflict and do what is best for the team and for himself. With this style or approach to your story, you have in effect created a "drama."

Again, your point of view might be neither of the above. You might want to show your ball game as a series of funny movements: players colliding with one another, one batter

The Educational Film:
   The Andes
                                                    Courtesy McGraw-Hill Films

The Educational Film:
Measuring (Science Processes Series) *Courtesy McGraw-Hill Films*

striking out six times in a row instead of three, a base runner moving in very slow motion from one base to another, the pitcher getting ready in a windup that never seems to end. With this as your approach, you have determined that the overall style of your plan will be "fantasy."

Finally, you decide you do not want to do any of these things. Instead, you would like to explain the fundamentals of the game to someone who knows nothing or very little about it. You want to acquaint your audience with the basic rules of the game, and perhaps show them how certain skills are developed, such as batting and pitching. With such an approach, the general idea is to get across the information to your viewer in as clear and succinct a way as possible. You might say that you are making a "how-to" film or, although this hardly shows the limits of the form, an "educational" movie.

As intimated before, filmmaking is not done arbitrarily or in the abstract. It is built upon one's personal experiences in life and upon how one feels about those experiences. There is something inside you that draws you to a particular subject, and once you decide to use that subject, you must find a suitable filmic design for it. This filmic form is the way you choose to express your subject so that the audience can experience your own feelings about it.

When you have chosen the overall style to use in approaching your subject, it is a good idea to put this plan on paper. The plan can take many forms, and the form that will serve you best in shooting is the one to select. You may then write a "treatment," which may be nothing more than several paragraphs in length, or even one paragraph, for that matter. You may write a "shooting treatment," which will be more detailed in terms of sequences and, sometimes, even specific shots. You may design a full "shooting script," which will list your shots in detail, as well as all the elements on your sound track. Or you may decide that your film form does not require you to be this elaborate. You might do nothing more than create a list that will supply you with the continuity for telling your story. As an example, take a look at the "plan" a sixth grader created for his film called *Feet*. It may look like nothing more than a list to us, but for him it provided a shooting script.

FEET *

A Film Script

by Michael Owen, 6th Grade

What are feet?
Feet with shoes—socks—stockings—bare

* Courtesy: The Collegiate School for Boys, New York, N.Y.

Feet getting on buses
Coming down stairs
Kicking
Running
Walking
Climbing
Feet in the shower—in the bath
Animal feet
Pigs' feet in the delicatessen
Feet on the moon (use of stills)
Feet swimming
Little feet, big feet
Footprints
Drawings of feet
Feet as measurement
A foot—several feet

A "treatment" is generally a written description of how one would treat the subject. Very often treatments are written by professional scriptwriters before they start on a detailed script. A treatment is a kind of visual outline of the film, and it can vary in length. A "shooting treatment" is often used by the professional documentary film maker; although he photographs events as they take place, he usually works from a detailed plan arising from his previous research on the subject. After he studies his subject in the preplanning stages, he evolves a shooting treatment that expresses his general conclusions on the subject. This allows for things to happen spontaneously on location, but imposes a cohesive attack or direction on the material as a whole. A shooting treatment generally lists the filming sequences or scenes that the film maker wishes to cover and suggests possible camera angles for executing them.

Let us say you have decided to make a film about the city, and that you specifically wish to show the city as a noisy, bustling place, as a place full of contrasts and injustices. Your treatment might look something like this:

A TALE OF TWO CITIES

(Treatment for a film on a large city)

We open on a very wide vista of a large metropolis. This is followed by a series of shots emphasizing largeness—crowds of people on the street, tall buildings shot from a very low angle (they seem to tower over us), people coming and going from the subway entrances. We hear loud traffic noises on our track, and then we see myriads of cars coming toward our camera. We hear sounds of footsteps and people talking. We see reflections of cars and people in the windows of glass buildings. We hear the sounds of ticker-tape machines and cash registers. We see shots of bank buildings, windows of department stores.

Suddenly, we see a child sitting alone on the steps of a tenement. Then we cut back to a crowd eating in a restaurant, women coming out of a department store with packages. We cut back to the same child walking alone through a vacant lot. He looks up toward a fire escape of one of the tenements. There is a pigeon on it. The pigeon takes flight.

We dissolve to a seagull in flight, and follow him as he eventually lands on a sandy stretch of beach. We see the ocean and can hear the waves and the gentle surf.

We cut back to the noisy city, with a montage of shots of windows, bars, fire escapes, traffic jams.

We cut to the child again. Now he is on the roof of a building. He looks out over the city.

We cut to a seagull in flight as it moves higher and higher and farther away from our camera.

As you would probably gather, a lot of different things could happen if you used this treatment as a basis for your film, and the eventual product might be considerably different from your plan. But the treatment would still be your original way of seeing and reacting to the subject of the city, and of expressing your feelings about it.

One thing to remember when you write the plan for your film is that film itself is the ideal viewer, and that in a plan —no matter what form it takes—you are breaking down the action into component pieces. Later, in your editing process, you will take these same components and put them together.

There are three basic kinds of shots that you should become familiar with: the close-up (CU), the medium shot (MS), and the long shot (LS). Their names indicate how far the camera is from the subject.

In a close-up, of course, we are very close to the subject; in a medium shot we are farther away; and in a long shot we are farther away still. These distances are relative, depending on the content you want for any given scene. A close-up can be a person's face or his entire torso. A medium shot can be of only one person, or of several. A long shot can be something relatively nearby or very far away. Relating close-ups, medium shots, and long shots gives life and variety to films. Fifteen seconds of a boy riding a bicycle is much less interesting than this same amount of time in which we first see a foot pedaling, then a smiling face, and finally a boy racing his bicycle along a country road (the latter shot perhaps taken from behind a cluster of tree leaves).

Suppose you want to photograph a city street. You might begin the sequence with an overall shot of people, cars, and shops. Then you cut to a medium shot that shows fewer details—maybe people walking by the shops. Finally you cut to a close-up of a single face. By giving each shot a different screen time, you give pace to the sequence.

Another important technique to remember is the "cutaway"—a shot that leaves the main action of the sequence but is generally related to it. For example, if you were doing a "sync"-sound segment, and filming a speaker addressing a group, you might also want to take cutaways of individual people in the speaker's audience. Or if you were

The close-up (CU); the medium shot (MS); the long shot (LS)

shooting your baseball game, you might want to take cut-aways of the fans in the bleachers applauding or yelling. If you were shooting two children playing ball on the beach, you might want to have some cutaways of just the waves and the surf itself, or perhaps of a nearby fisherman.

The intention you wish to express in your film can be altered by the location of your camera in relation to the sequence action. This we refer to as camera angle. Shooting from different camera angles can add a great amount of excitement to your film. Camera angle does not mean how far the camera is positioned from the subject, but from what angle or viewpoint it shoots it. For example, if you were to shoot a fistfight taking place in a field, you might choose any number of angles, depending upon what you want to say cinematically about the fight. If you shot the fight from a high angle (the window of a nearby building), you might create an interesting perspective on the fight, but it would hardly have much of an emotional impact upon your viewers. On the other hand, if you lay on the ground with your camera and shot up into the faces of the boys fighting (preferably with a wide-angle lens), the battle would be much more dynamic. Again, suppose you wanted to make your audience feel that they were almost a part of the fight. You might then position your camera opposite one of the boys and ask him to throw his punches directly at it. Whatever angle you choose, remember that you are not limited to that angle for the entire sequence. Assuming that the fight is your "whole"—a whole is made up of component parts— you can combine all of these camera angles when you shoot your fight.

You can control what the audience sees and also make very effective use of your zoom lens by revealing a scene gradually. In many cases this approach adds the element of suspense to a shot (you may have seen it used in feature films that are thrillers or detective stories). The shot begins on a person seated on a fence with his back to the camera. After a moment's hold we begin to zoom back slowly. As we do, we reveal the barrel of a gun, apparently aimed at the person on the fence. Then we zoom back even more and reveal the face of another person who has the sight of his rifle cocked next to his eye. By attacking the scene in this way—by permitting the audience to see only what you wish to reveal to them—surprise and tension are added to the sequence.

In addition to presenting an event by degrees, another way to put life in your sequence is to bring people or things suddenly into your frame of view or out of it. For example, let's look at a Hollywood thriller. Someone is walking along the street toward the camera. It is dark and all we hear is footsteps. The camera is steadily positioned on a long shot of the walking person. He gets closer and closer to the lens. Suddenly, when the figure is practically full-frame, a hand enters the frame from the left and grabs the shoulder of the walking person. He is surprised—and certainly so is the audience!

So far the techniques that we have been talking about

involve only a steady camera in one position. But there are other effects that can be achieved by *moving* your camera. Four of the possibilities are the *pan* shot, the *tilt,* the *dolly,* and the *tracking* shot.

For the pan and the tilt, it is important that you keep your camera on a tripod that has a good pan head, so you can achieve the desired smoothness in movement. A pan is the movement across the frame, from right to left or left to right. A tilt is the movement up or down the frame. In other words, the pan is a horizontal movement and the tilt a vertical movement. You can pan across a single subject without having that subject move, or you can reveal that subject at the end of a pan. You might pan from left to right, let us say, if you were doing a sequence on fishing. You would perhaps begin your shot on the water and keep moving your camera right until you finally settled on a fisherman standing on a dock in the right of your frame. If you were photographing a tug-of-war game, you might position your camera on a tripod in the center of the field. Then you would begin your pan on the group at the left, and keep moving your camera right until you had revealed the group tugging on the right.

Suppose you wanted to show a child with a puppy. You might begin your shot with a close-up of the child's face and then gradually *tilt* your camera down until you revealed the puppy the child held in his arms. Or you could reverse the action, tilting *up* from the puppy to the child. You might use the same device if you were photographing a tree that was practically barren of all leaves. You would begin your shot on the branches of the tree and then tilt down to show the brightly colored autumn leaves on the ground beneath it.

Dollying usually means moving into an object or pulling back (or moving away) from it. Professionally, there are many kinds of dolly mounts, and they mainly require a smooth surface on which to move. Chances are you will not be

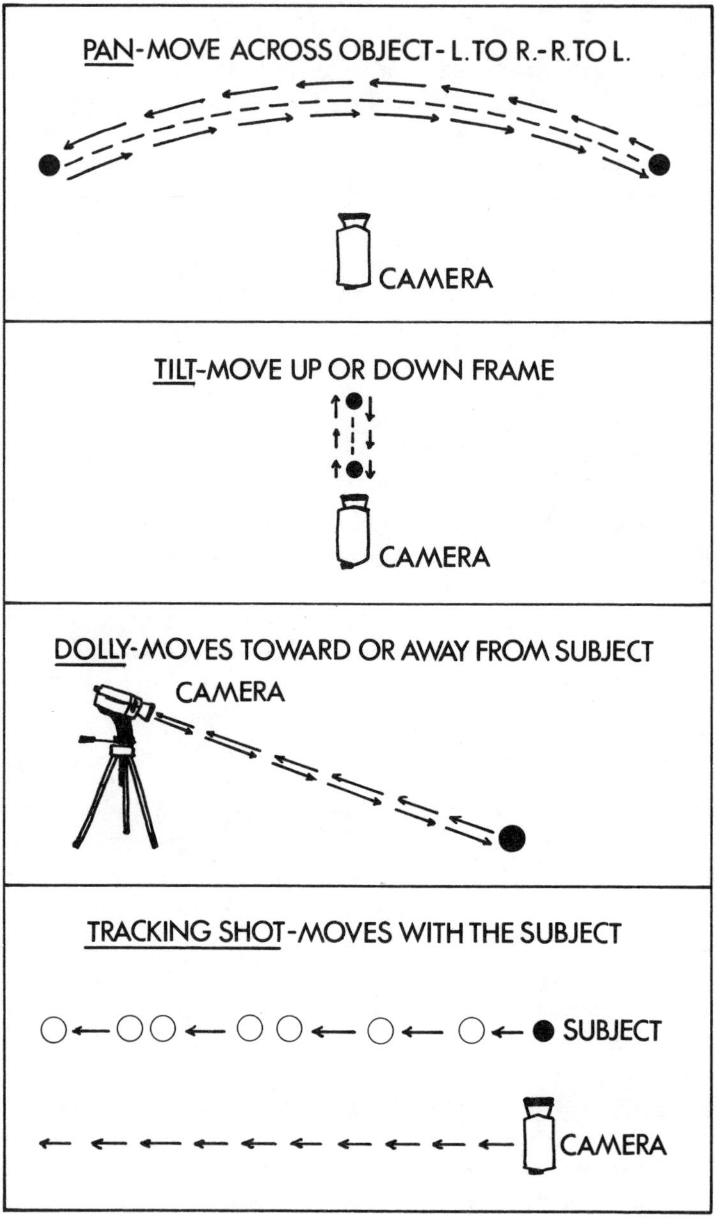

PAN-MOVE ACROSS OBJECT- L. TO R.- R. TO L.

CAMERA

TILT-MOVE UP OR DOWN FRAME

CAMERA

DOLLY-MOVES TOWARD OR AWAY FROM SUBJECT

CAMERA

TRACKING SHOT-MOVES WITH THE SUBJECT

SUBJECT

CAMERA

working with such mounts, but that does not mean you cannot improvise your own kind of dolly. For one thing, your zoom lens can almost give you the same effect. You might start with a close-up of a bee, then pull back to reveal the flower it is on, and then—still in the same smooth, continuous movement—reveal the entire garden of flowers. Using your body as a brace, and after much practice, you will be able to "walk" a dolly. Let us say you want to dolly in toward a doorway of a home. With your camera in hand, you can simply walk toward the doorway, shooting as you go.

A tracking shot means that you "track" with your subject, that is, you and your camera move with him. Again, there are elaborate professional devices for tracking, but you can improvise your own. With a bit of ingenuity you can move your camera along with the action, thus involving the audience directly in it. Instead of looking at the action, they are made to feel that they are a part of it.

For example, some friends of yours are having a bicycle race and you want to shoot it; you also want to create a sense of "being there." The best way is for you to become part of the action—have the camera move along with it. Get a friend and a bicycle, and position yourself on the crossbars of the bike. Stay on one side of the racing group, and as they move, you and your friend move with them. Hold your camera as steady as possible on the action next to you, and try to stay just slightly to the fore of it. You can also track by walking with the moving object (providing it does not exceed your speed and you can walk very steadily).

Speaking of improvising, you are not the only one who does such a thing. One of the favorite dollying and tracking devices for a lot of directors and/or cameramen is the wheelchair! The photographer merely sits in the chair and handholds the camera while an assistant pushes him. This device has proved to be very versatile and effective.

These, then, are some of the techniques and the tools you will use. Knowing your tools will help you make your plan—

to write the treatment or script—after you have decided on your subject and how you want to present it. To make a good, workable plan, you must be able to think filmically. In your mind, your imagination, you must be able to break down your subject into sequences and visualize these sequences in relation to each other. Further, you must be able to see each shot in relation to the others. And even within each shot, you must be able to see the relationship between one object and another. Knowing how to achieve these component elements can help you orchestrate your film— put your pieces together in such a way that they will express your exact intention.

On the next few pages you will find a sample of an actual shooting script. It is a drama as well as an educational film, and was created not only to tell a story, but also to encourage children to write stories of their own. It was produced by ACI Films, Inc. as part of their "Read On!" Film Series.

AND THEN WHAT HAPPENED? *

(SHOOTING SCRIPT)

1. In back we hear piano music—nickelodeon style. After a beat, a title card comes on with the company credit (in flourishy letters, tinted slightly sepia on black—like a silent film). That title card is replaced by a second one: AND THEN WHAT HAPPENED? The second title card is replaced by a third: STARRING DONNA, JESSE, AND YOU . . .

Central Narrator

2. AFTER TITLES OUT, CUT TO LIVE ACTION. LS, AS CAMERA DREAM-ILY EXPLORES SMALL FARM, MOV-ING OVER THE DISTANT VISTA,

Donna and Jesse lived on a farm. It was not a big farm, but it had chickens, a horse named Henry, a large, furry

* Courtesy of ACI Films, Inc. From the "Read On!" Series, copyright 1971 by ACI Films.

AND THEN MOVING IN FOR TIGHTER SHOTS: CHICKENS STRUTTING NEAR COOP, HORSE MUNCHING ON GRASS NEXT TO BARN, A LARGE, FURRY DOG LYING LAZILY IN THE SUN, AND DUCKS SWIMMING IN A POND.

dog called Barnaby, and ducks that swam in a pond nearby.

3. CUT TO CU, EIGHT-YEAR-OLD GIRL ACCOMPANIED BY FOUR-YEAR-OLD-GIRL. FOUR-YEAR-OLD IS IN A PLAY DRESS, AND EIGHT-YEAR IS IN A PLAY TOP AND BLUE JEANS. CAMERA FOLLOWS THEM AS OLDER ONE THROWS OUT FEED TO THE CHICKENS, THEN COLLECTS EGGS (MS) FROM HENS IN COOP.

After school and on Saturdays, Donna did chores on the farm. She fed the chickens.

CUT TO OLDER ONE, STILL FOLLOWED AND SOMETIMES AIDED BY YOUNGER ONE. PICKS APPLES FROM LOW-LYING BRANCHES OF TREES, AND PLACES THEM IN BASKET.

She collected the fresh eggs from the chicken coop, and picked the fruit from the trees. Jesse was too small to do any chores yet, but she followed Donna around, and pretended that she, too, was working on the farm.

CU OF RATHER EXASPERATED LOOK ON OLDER GIRL'S FACE AS SHE RELATES TO HER YOUNGER SISTER.

CUT TO WIDER SHOT. DONNA IS IMPATIENTLY THROWING OUT THE ROTTEN APPLES THAT JESSE HAS PUT INTO THE BASKET (TRYING TO BE HELPFUL). DONNA ATTEMPTS TO EXPLAIN THAT SHE DOESN'T WANT THE APPLES THAT ARE LYING ON THE GROUND. IN CU SHE

Donna loved her little sister Jesse, but she was not very happy when Jesse tagged after her all the time. She would always sigh with exasperation when their mother would say, "Now keep an eye on Jesse. Watch that she doesn't get into any trouble." Donna liked doing the chores, but she didn't like being a baby-sitter for her own sister. Especially

SHOWS JESSE THAT THEY HAVE BEEN PARTIALLY EATEN BY WORMS.

since Jesse was forever getting into trouble.

4. CUT TO SERIES OF SHOTS, HAZY RENDERINGS OF MEMORY, EDGES OF FRAME SLIGHTLY BLURRED: LITTLE JESSE IN CORNFIELD, STALKS ALL ABOUT HER, AND SHE MAKING SEVERAL ATTEMPTS TO FIND HER WAY OUT;

Twice she got lost in the cornfield,

LOW-ANGLE (FROM BOTTOM OF LADDER), JESSE AT TOP OF HAYLOFT LOOKING DOWN FORLORNLY;

and another time she climbed the ladder to the top of the hayloft.

MS, JESSE TRIPPING WITH EGG-FILLED BASKET IN CHICKEN COOP, AND EGGS BREAKING BENEATH AND AROUND HER; JESSE, NEAR HOUSE WITH DOG, DIPPING FINGERS OF ONE HAND INTO PAINTS AND RUBBING THEM ONTO PATIENT, TOLERANT ANIMAL.

Once, she broke sixteen eggs when Donna let her hold the egg basket in the chicken coop. Of course, that wasn't as bad as the time she tried to paint Barnaby red and blue with finger paints.

5. MS, TWO GIRLS ABOUT THE SAME AGE AS DONNA.
WIDEN SHOT TO SHOW DONNA, TWO GIRLS CARRYING GAME EQUIPMENT FROM THE HOUSE. THREE ARE WALKING TOGETHER. REVERSE ANGLE TO SHOW JESSE TRAILING BEHIND THEM.

When Donna's friends came for a visit one Saturday afternoon, Jesse was very pleased to have company.

CU OF DONNA'S FACE, GROWING PERTURBED.
CUT TO WIDER SHOT. DONNA MOVES FROM HER FRIENDS. FACES JESSE AND ADMONISHES HER. THEN SHE GESTURES FOR JESSE TO

She tagged along after them until Donna could stand it no longer. "Everyone knows," Donna told Jesse angrily, "that little girls can't play the same games as big girls can. Go

LEAVE HER AND HER FRIENDS.

CU OF JESSE'S RATHER SAD AND ASHAMED FACE.
MS OF TWO SISTERS IN CONVERSATION. MLS (medium long shot), DONNA TURNS AWAY FROM JESSE, AND WITH HER FRIENDS AND EQUIPMENT BEGINS MOVING TOWARD CAMERA.
WE CAN SEE JESSE IN BACKGROUND OF FRAME.
ZOOM IN TOWARD JESSE, LOOKING FORLORNLY AT CAMERA (AS IF AT HER SISTER AND HER SISTER'S FRIENDS—IN FOREGROUND).
JESSE TURNS AROUND AND MOVES AWAY FROM CAMERA INTO THE DISTANCE.

6. CUT TO SERIES OF EXHILARATING SHOTS OF THREE OLDER GIRLS PLAYING GAME OF PITCHING BEAN-BAGS INTO MOUTH OF CLOWN-PAINTED BOARD (GAME IS VERY MUCH CHILD'S VERSION OF QUOITS). VISUALS EMPHASIZE DONNA, INTERCUT WITH HER

away, pest," she added sternly. "I'm not your baby-sitter! Why can't you get your own friends and play with them?"
Jesse looked up at her sister sadly. "How can I find friends?" she asked. "I'm not old enough to go to school,

and the house near ours only has big kids in it." But Donna paid no attention to Jesse's complaint.

Oh well, thought Jesse, there's always Henry and Barnaby.

Then, little Jesse wandered off by herself, wishing that some magical act could make her as old as Donna. If that happened, though, she thought with glee, she would have her own friends—and she wasn't quite sure whether or not she would let Donna play with them.
Donna entertained her friends with her new bean-bag game. She was a very good bean-bag player. She won four games in a row—until she was absolute champion.

Just as they were about to be-

WINNING TOSSES.
MS OF JESSE GETTING INTO BOAT AT EDGE OF DUCK POND. DOG BARNABY IS ALREADY IN THE BOAT.
CU OF JESSE HAPPILY HUGGING BARNABY.
CUT BACK TO DONNA AND HER FRIENDS. DONNA PUTS DOWN HER BEAN-BAGS.
FRIENDS PUT DOWN THEIRS AND VOLUNTEER TO HELP DONNA.
CU OF ONE OF FRIENDS AS SHE NODS HER HEAD AS DONNA SPEAKS TO HER.
CU OF OTHER FRIEND AS SHE DOES SAME THING.
LS, AS THREE GIRLS SEPARATE AND MOVE IN DIFFERENT DIRECTIONS.
MS OF DONNA AS SHE WALKS, LOOKS APPREHENSIVELY, AND CALLS JESSE'S NAME.

CUT TO CU OF ROPE THAT ANCHORS POND BOAT TO MOORING SLIPPING LOOSE. ROPE SLIPS COMPLETELY NOW. CUT TO WIDER SHOT AS BOAT, UNANCHORED, BEGINS TO MOVE SLOWLY OUT TOWARD MIDDLE OF THE POND, CARRYING JESSE AND BARNABY WITH IT.
CUT BACK TO DONNA FROM BEHIND HER, COMING UPON DUCK

gin another game, Donna realized that she hadn't seen pesty Jesse for over an hour. "Jesse?" she called. There was no answer.
Again she called, and again no answer.
"I'd better find that dumb Jesse," she told her friends, "before she gets into trouble." The friends volunteered to help in the search.
"You go to the cornfield," Donna told Nancy,

"and you," she said to Marie, "take a look in the hayloft." The three girls separated.

Donna called Jesse's name as she walked. Of course, she couldn't call too loudly. Their mother might hear, and get very worried that Jesse was lost.
Donna looked in the chicken coop. No, Jesse was not with the chickens. She wasn't with Henry. And Barnaby was nowhere in sight.

Not until she came to the duck pond did Donna see Jesse.

POND. QUICK ZOOM INTO BOAT IN MIDDLE OF POND.
QUICK REVERSE ZOOM BACK INTO SURPRISED FACE OF DONNA.

7. TITLE CARD SLIPS ON:
OH! OH! JESSE IS MAROONED IN THE MIDDLE OF THE POND.

CUT BACK TO LIVE ACTION. MS, DONNA RUNNING TO EDGE OF POND, SHOUTING TO HER SISTER.
TITLE CARD SLIPS ON:
BUT HOW?
CUT BACK TO LIVE ACTION AND CU OF DONNA'S REMORSEFUL FACE.
TITLE CARD SLIPS ON:
I KNOW. I'LL GET MY FRIENDS TO HELP.
CUT TO LIVE ACTION. VISUALS ARE VERY QUICK AND IN SPEEDED-UP ACTION, REPRESENTING THE THOUGHTS OF THE HEROINE. MOSTLY IN LONG SHOTS, WE SEE HER RACING TO HER FRIEND IN THE CORNFIELD, THEN BOTH OF THEM RACING TO THE OTHER FRIEND IN THE HAYLOFT, AND THEN ALL THREE RACING TO THE DUCK POND TOGETHER.
TITLE CARD SLIPS ON:
I'LL SWIM TO THE BOAT MYSELF.
AGAIN ACTION IS IN HIGH SPEED.
DONNA RACES TO HER BEDROOM,

There, in the boat, in the middle of the pond, was her little sister with Barnaby.
(MENACING MUSIC UP— PLAYER PIANO IN STYLE OF OLD MOVIES)

"Oh! Oh!", cried Donna. "Jesse is marooned in the middle of the pond."
"Don't worry, Jesse," Donna shouted to her sister. "I'll save you!"

"But how?"
"I'm sorry I called you a pest," Donna shouted. And she really meant it.

"I know. I'll get my friends to help," thought Donna.
(MUSIC UP TO MATCH SPEEDED-UP RESCUE ACTIVITY)

"I'll swim to the boat myself."

PUTS ON HER LIFE JACKET, AND
THEN SWIMS FURIOUSLY WITH IT
OUT TOWARD BOAT.

(MUSIC UP)

CUT BACK TO LIVE ACTION.
DONNA SPOTS ROPE NEAR MOOR-
ING. ZOOM INTO CU OF ROPE.

TITLE CARD SLIPS ON:

*I'LL THROW OUT THE ROPE AND
PULL THE BOAT TO SHORE.*

"I'll throw out the rope and
pull the boat to shore."

CUT TO SPEEDED-UP ACTION.
DONNA RUNNING TO ROPE AT
MOORING AND THEN TRYING TO
TOSS IT TO JESSE AND BARNABY.

(MUSIC UP)

TITLE CARD SLIPS ON:

*I'LL RIDE OUT ON HENRY, AND TO-
GETHER WE'LL RESCUE JESSE.*

"I'll ride out on Henry, and
together we'll rescue Jesse."

CUT TO SPEEDED-UP ACTION
AGAIN. DONNA RUNNING TO
FIELD BEHIND BARN, MOUNTING
HENRY WITH A FLOURISH, AND
RIDING BACK TO THE RESCUE.

(MUSIC UP)

CUT BACK TO REALISTIC DONNA,
PACING THE SHORELINE OF THE
POND, WATCHING HER SISTER IN
THE BOAT.

"No," thought Donna, "I'll
just walk to the boat. I'll walk
in the water. But I don't know
how deep the water is."

SHE LOOKS AROUND ON THE
SHORE. SUBJECTIVE SHOT AS CAM-
ERA MOVES OVER THE GROUND
AROUND THE MOORING SPOT.

"Where is the oar?" she asked
herself as she looked around.
"Maybe I can reach Jesse with
the oar."

TIGHT SHOT OF BOAT INTERIOR:
JESSE, BARNABY, AND TILT DOWN
TO OAR.

Alas, the oar was in the boat
with Jesse and Barnaby. Then
Donna had another idea.

TITLE CARD SLIPS ON:

*I'LL WAIT FOR THE WIND TO
MOVE THE BOAT TO THE SHORE.
THEN I'LL GRAB HOLD OF THE*

"I'll wait for the wind to
move the boat to the shore.
Then I'll grab hold of the

BOAT.

CUT TO SPEEDED-UP VISUALS. AGAIN, DONNA'S FANTASY. SHE RACES AROUND TO DIFFERENT POINTS ON THE SHORE, TRYING TO ANTICIPATE THE MOVEMENT OF THE WIND AT EACH. (AT EACH POINT SHE LIES FLAT ON SHORE, GETTING INTO A POSITION TO GRAB BOAT IF IT COMES SAILING TOWARD HER.)

CUT BACK TO REALITY. DONNA IS WATCHING JESSE IN THE BOAT. CAMERA FOLLOWS MOVEMENT AS SHE LOOKS TOWARD THE SKY.

TITLE CARD SLIPS ON:

WHAT WILL HAPPEN IF IT BEGINS TO RAIN?

CUT BACK TO REALISTIC LIVE ACTION. MS OF DONNA WAVING

HER ARM AT JESSE.

CU OF JESSE AND BARNABY IN THE BOAT, JESSE LOOKING HELPLESS AND ON THE VERGE OF TEARS.

TIGHT CU OF BARNABY.

LS OF NANCY SEARCHING CORN-FIELD.

MS OF MARIE SEARCHING HAY-LOFT.

boat."

(MUSIC UP)

"But what if no wind comes?" Donna thought.

"What will happen if it begins to rain?"

"Jesse, come back," Donna shouted. "I want you to play with me and my friends—our friends!"

Jesse and Barnaby sat looking very unhappy in the boat in the middle of the pond. "I want to go home," Jesse whimpered.

"Arrrrrhhhhhh," Barnaby whined from the boat.

(MUSIC)

"Jesse? Jesse?" Nancy called in the cornfield.

(MUSIC)

"Jesse? Jesse?" Marie called in the hayloft.

(MUSIC)

LS OF DONNA ON SHORE (TAKEN FROM OTHER SIDE).	"I'll save you, Jesse," shouted Donna from the shore of the duck pond. (MUSIC)
TITLE CARD SLIPS ON: *WHAT WILL HAPPEN TO POOR LIT-TLE JESSE?*	What will happen to poor little Jesse?

8. Screen goes to black for a full beat, and then we introduce the three different endings to the film that have been created by the children themselves. We hear their voices on the track as they very spontaneously narrate their own conclusions for the story—some logical, some very fanciful, and perhaps some very zany. The visuals can be simple animation, taken from the drawings of children themselves. Music can continue to be piano, or can come out of the style of the individual child's conclusion—a different instrument for each ending (violin, drum, flute, etc.).

9. After children's contributions, conclusions, and narrations are over, we cut to live action visual of Jesse and Barnaby and boat bobbing in the middle of the pond.

	There are many ways to end a story, and there are many kinds of stories. Who knows what happened to poor little Jesse?
TITLE CARD SLIPS ON: *DO YOU?*	Do you?
FADE OUT, AND GO TO SIMPLE WHITE ON BLACK FOR TAIL ACI CREDITS.	(PIANO MUSIC UP FOR FLOURISH)

As you can see from the previous script, visual details have been incorporated into shots of a much wider and more general nature. Shots have varied in camera angle and in screen direction. Remember when you shoot or even prepare a plan, you are controlling what you want the audience to see at a given time.

The treatment and script incorporate certain filmmaking tools that you need to know if you are to be in control of your product. These tools will help you achieve the filmic form that expresses your intention.

CHAPTER 6

Shooting Your Film

In a sense, the director is the author of a film. He is responsible for the overall production. He not only directs the actors, he also oversees the photography, the lighting, the costuming, and the set. Very often he is at least coauthor of the script. It is the director's film sense that ultimately establishes the film's form. He "calls the shot," decides on the camera angles, supervises editing and soundwork. The final film is the outgrowth of his personal filmic vision, and this is true whether the director is a highly paid professional working with a multitude of assistants, technicians, and various artisans, or an individual single film maker who does his own scripting, shooting, and editing.

As the director of your film, you will first consider the lighting. Not only must the subject be seen, but lighting also creates an atmosphere. By lighting subjects fully and directly, you will get a bright effect. By lighting them only partially, you can achieve mysterious, suspenseful effects. By using only "available" light sources, you will get a more realistic look.

When you are shooting outdoors, you will probably want to use as much sunlight as possible. The results will depend upon how you move your subject in relation to this source. A primary point to bear in mind about outdoor lighting is that you should try to keep the contrast on your subject to a minimum—that is, the light and dark areas should not be so starkly different that they are unpleasant or distracting. One side of a subject's face may be brightly lit by the sun and the other side be in dark shadow. To even this out and reduce the contrast, you might use a reflector, which would bounce the light from the sun onto the subject. A reflector can heighten the skin tone of a human subject and add a glossy look to the eyes. Direct it or aim it just as you would a mirror. Of course, elaborate professional reflectors do exist, but you can make your own by taking a large piece of cardboard and covering it completely with aluminum foil.

Most of the time you will illuminate your subjects from the front, but an excellent and increasingly used technique is backlighting. In this technique the sunlight is behind the subject, not in front of him, creating a very pretty effect. A backlighted subject will have a soft glow or halo, with highlights particularly on his hair. This type of lighting is especially good for young children, and is also used frequently these days in television commercials in which people are presented as being attractive and healthy.

When you are shooting indoors, remember that ordinary home lighting may be bright enough for your eyes but not strong enough to register an image on film (except for special circumstances, which will be discussed later). In this case you will have to use movie lights. Some cameras come equipped with devices for attaching a light directly to them. Other lights that you can use are photo lamps with built-in reflectors, which screw into a light bar or into light sockets attached to clamps. You can also use a sealed-beam light or a tungsten-halogen lamp.

In working with indoor movie lights, it is necessary to use both the right film and the right exposure. You cannot use the regular daylight-type film indoors with lights because your exposed film will then have an orange cast to it. The distance between your subject and the light source is also important during exposure. The brighter your subject (the nearer to the light), the smaller the lens opening; the dimmer your subject (the farther from the light), the larger your lens opening.

A camera with an automatic exposure control will set the

Subject with sharp, ugly contrasts.

A homemade reflector used on the same subject removes much of the contrast.

The same subject backlighted.

INDOOR EXPOSURE TABLE
FOR KODACHROME MOVIE FILM, TYPE A

Lens Opening	650-Watt Tungsten-Halogen Movie Light Flood Beam	650-Watt Tungsten-Halogen Movie Light Spot Beam	650-Watt Sealed-Beam Movie Light	2-Lamp Light Bar with 300- or 375-Watt Reflector Photo Lamps
F 8	6 feet	6–9 feet	4–5½ feet	3½–5 feet
F 5.6	6–9 feet	9–12 feet	5½–8 feet	5–7 feet
F 4	9–12 feet	12–17 feet	8–11 feet	7–10 feet
F 2.8	12–17 feet	17–24 feet	11–16 feet	10–14 feet
F 1.9	17–24 feet	24–35 feet	16–24 feet	14–21 feet

proper lens opening for you automatically with indoor lights just as it does outdoors. But if you must set the exposure control yourself, and you do not have a light meter, follow the recommendations that come with your movie lights or photo lamps. You can also use the following table as a general guide.

You can aim your movie lights directly at your subject, but much more pleasing effects can be achieved if you bounce the light onto your subject. Most movie lights tilt up so that you can aim them at the ceiling. In bounce lighting, your light hits the ceiling between your camera and your subject, and thus reflects the illumination over a wider area, removing any harsh shadows. Bounced light is much softer than direct lighting, and because it illuminates a larger area, you usually do not have to change exposure each time you move your subject. In addition, you will find that bounced light is much easier on your subject's eyes. Consequently, there should be no squinting into the lens.

Sometimes bounced light is added to the existing light in the room. As such, it fills in shadows, makes them less harsh, and greatly lessens any undesirable contrast. A word of caution: Try not to use bounced light on a colored ceiling. If you do, the color of the ceiling will most likely be reflected onto your subject. In choosing exposure for bounced light, you can generally rely on the rule of using a lens opening two stops larger than that which you would use for direct lighting at the same distance from your subject.

If you can afford to use two lights instead of one on your subject, you will get a much more professional, much more pleasing effect. In this case, place your main light from two to four feet higher than your second light, and position it at a 45-degree angle from the line between the subject and the camera.

Place your second, fill-in light on the other side of the camera and at the same distance from the subject as the main light. Using two lights in this way creates highlights

Exposing for the water put the tree in silhouette and made day seem like night.

Photo by Stemm

and depth, and very natural-looking results.

With the new high-speed color film, you can also take indoor movies with "available" or existing light without using movie lights—if you have a camera that can accommodate this. Existing light may be light from table lamps, or coming through a window, or from candles or a fireplace. These existing-light sequences can be filmed much more quickly, and chances are that your subjects will be much more at ease. With an existing-light movie camera and high-speed film, you can even take some very exciting filmic sequences outdoors at night, although it is recommended that you concentrate on subjects that already have some interesting light available—for example, the amusement park, a

scene of fireworks, or Christmas decorations outdoors in the city.

A concern about composition will certainly enhance the quality of your shooting, but perfecting it will take practice and you may make many mistakes, as in any other craft. There are certain rules, however, that should help you make better-composed shots.

First of all, remember that each shot should have a single center of interest. Decide what it is in the shot that you want to attract your viewer's eye to, and make it your focal center. This not only makes for a cleaner shot, it also keeps your intention clear. If you have several things in the shot "fighting" each other for your viewer's interest, you will ultimately get only his lack of interest.

Second, try to keep the background of your shot as simple and uncluttered as possible. These background elements, unless intentionally planned, will only distract from your

Without proper screen direction, the boy on the bicycle appears to be racing toward himself.

center of interest. Always test your shot in the viewfinder of your camera before you begin shooting.

Finally, try to keep your horizons and your subjects level, unless you want to create a special, distorted effect. A good way to present your subject is with a natural framing device such as an arch or foliage. Natural framing will also add depth to your shot.

A director must always remember to match the direction of all action on the screen. Unless that is done in shooting a film, the editing will be very difficult, and the result could be confusing to the audience. For example, suppose that when shooting a boy riding a bicycle from screen right to screen left (these directions are from the camera's point of view), the director took a medium shot of the boy on his bicycle and then a close-up of the boy's face. If he took the latter from the opposite side of the original camera position, he would find, when he went to assemble his film in editing, that his shots did not "match"—i.e., they were in an opposite screen direction. The boy and bike in the first shot would be moving from screen right to screen left; the boy's face in the second shot would be moving from screen left to screen right. The effect would be that the boy was moving toward himself.

Another example of maintaining proper screen direction is in a conversation between two people. Let us say a boy and a girl were talking to each other, and you were filming their conversation as they sat looking at each other in profile. The girl was on the left-hand side of the screen, the boy on the right. You shot a "master shot" of the two—that is, an overall shot of the complete action of the scene. Then you decided to shoot close-ups. But this time you moved your camera to photograph the girl from the side opposite that of the master shot. If, when you cut the film, you placed the master shot in front of the close-up of the girl, it would appear that in the first shot she was talking to the boy, and that in the second shot (the CU), she was talking to herself. Again, the audience would be confused, because the shots would not "match" in screen direction.

Although you have established screen direction, you can still always change it. Sometimes changing screen direction will be exactly what you want to do to fulfill your cinematic intention, but doing so usually requires the use of a bridging or transitional shot or shots. Returning to our example of the boy on the bicycle, let us say the first shot is the same—boy and bicycle moving from screen right to screen left. You can change the screen direction by taking a second shot of the boy and the bicycle coming directly toward the camera (a "head-on" shot). Then you will be able to shoot a third shot from the opposite side of the first one, and it will not be confusing because you have inserted another shot with a neutral screen direction.

"Matching" the action means controlling the continuity of your film. In addition to keeping the screen direction similar, you must also see that the size of moving objects is the same in successive shots, that their color or texture is similar, and that their rate of speed is essentially the same.

In shooting your film, remember that a variety of shots will add great vitality to the sequences, and will make them more dynamic as well as much more interesting to your audience. To return again to the example of the boy on the bicycle, this time imagine that you have decided you want to film a bicycle race. You want to involve the audience in the action as much as you can, and you want to create a sense of suspense as to who the winner will be.

First of all, you will probably have to shoot the same sequence several times, so it is important that you remember the positions of the cyclists at all times in order to match action and maintain continuity. You might begin with a master shot. The camera is positioned about 40 or 50 feet from the action for a long shot. The boys line up at the starting post. You begin to shoot the action several seconds before they actually begin to race. As they move, you "pan" with them, keeping the action centered in the frame, and you remain on the action until the race is completed at the finish line. Thus, with this master shot, you have recorded the entire sequence in one long shot.

Now, remembering the exact action of the sequence— who was ahead and when, etc.—you ask your cyclists to repeat the same thing again. This time, you and your camera are positioned next to the racers on the crossbars of another bike being driven by your assistant. The race begins, and your shot is a "tracking" shot; you are moving with the racers.

After this has been done, you put the racers through their paces once more. Now your camera is on a tripod at the finish line and you are using a telephoto lens. The race begins. You shoot a medium shot of the racers starting out, and as they move toward you, you shoot close-ups ("head-on") of each racer's face. Then you "pull back" with your telephoto lens and shoot the winner as he crosses the finish line and stops (at this point he should be very large in the frame—stopping just short of appearing to fall into the lap of the audience).

Once more, with this shot completed, you ask your racers to begin again. This time you are back on the bicycle of your friend and assistant, and several feet behind the racing cyclists, taking what is called a "reverse-angle" shot. You are moving slightly under the speed of the racers, and covering them from the rear in a medium shot.

Then, although you have certainly covered the action, you feel that just to be on the safe side you want to take a few more details that will give added dimension and vitality to the sequence. Here you can do any number of things. You can take "cutaways" that will make your editing of the sequence much more exciting and much less limited. Move in for a close-up of a bicycle wheel turning, its spokes perhaps catching reflections from the sun. Take a close-up of one of the racer's feet pedaling. "Tilt" down from a CU of a racer's face to a CU of his hands gripping the handle-bar of his bike (to accomplish these shots most effectively, you might have to be again driven by your friend-assistant on his bike).

Finally, you might want to do a "first-person," subjective shot, taken from the point of view of the cyclist who is losing the race. For this you will again have to be driven by your friend. Start up the race, but this time you and your camera have replaced the second (and losing) racer. Your camera is seeing the race from his point of view. It might be a good idea to frame this shot by having the handlebars of the bike in the lower fourth of the frame. Shoot straight ahead, keeping the racer ahead of you in part of the frame for most of your shot. This final shot should certainly give your audience a sense of "being there."

The following list shows the variety of shots that you have now taken to make this sequence come alive filmically.

These are the component pieces that you will put together later when you edit the film:

1) Master shot—LS—moving R. to L., pan with entire action
2) Tracking shot, moving R. to L. with cyclists
3) Head-on telephoto shot from behind finish line
       MS of start of race
       CU's of each racer's face
       Head-on MS to CU of winner crossing finish line
4) Reverse-angle MS dolly from behind racers
5) Cutaways
       CU of moving bicycle wheel
       CU of racer's foot pedaling
       Tilt down from CU of racer's face to CU of his hands gripping bike handlebar
6) First-person subjective moving MS from the point of view of the losing racer, keeping winning racer in part of the frame

As you can see, you shot only one sequence, but it took time, patience, and thinking to choose a variety of shots that would bring rhythm and pacing to the finished product. Also, you had to shoot the same sequence several times, and that probably took a great deal of patience and cooperation from your racers—or actors, in this case. This brings us to the final point in this chapter—how to direct people.

It is almost a certainty that at this stage of your work in film, you will not be working with any professional actors. Instead, you will be rounding up willing friends and asking them to play themselves or other characters in your films. First of all, remember that no one can really tell you how to direct your "actors"—whether they are strangers or friends. You are going to have to get the feel of it by yourself, by trial and error, by making mistakes and trying to correct them the next time around. Here are some suggestions, however, for working with nonactors.

An important thing to remember is that you should not *force* people to "act" in your film. Do not even try to convince them. Use only very willing volunteers who are eager to work with you, who have the time and the patience to do a scene over and over again. If you use someone who is only half-willing, you are apt to have a cast dropout. It is also best to use those friends of yours who also have an interest in films. Then they may appreciate some of your problems, and may even help you solve them on occasion. In addition, they might be able to assist you technically when they are not appearing in the scene as actors.

When you are working with your "actors," try not to kill their enthusiasm for what they are doing by being too rigid and demanding. Help keep up their spirit for the work by letting them feel that they are a vital part of it. If you ask them to perform some kind of action, let them practice it before you shoot, so that they will feel comfortable. After all, nobody wants to look foolishly awkward, and your actors need rehearsal as much as you do. It does not hurt at all to ask them if they have any personal suggestions that they would like to make about the scene you are doing. Keep your vision and intention firm in your head, but take the time to listen to what they have to say. This is not merely a courtesy. They may come up with something that is exciting and will complement your filmic intention.

When you want an actor friend to display a particular emotion, it is more effective if you are not too direct. Do not say, "I want you to laugh now" or "I want you to cry now." The result you want is naturalness. Your actors should not look like actors. Their behavior on the screen (and the motion-picture camera picks up behavioral fakery very easily) should appear realistic at all times—unless you are doing an obvious farce or parody.

If you want someone to laugh for a shot, you can do any number of things that will bring better results than the order: "Laugh now!" You might let the actor warm up by himself, or have another actor tell him a funny joke—and wait to shoot until he gives the appropriate natural response. You might even go so far as to have someone (even yourself) tickle him. Certainly this type of approach to behavior on the screen and working with actors will bring more believable results. If, for example, you want someone to look very tired and out of breath (he has just been chased by a ferocious lion), you might get the effect you want simply by asking him to run in place for about five minutes before you begin to shoot the scene. Whatever the emotional behavior you desire for a sequence, remember that you can and should think of ways to help the actor achieve it realistically.

If you are working with very small children, there is always the strong possibility that they will spend much of your shooting time looking into the lens of the camera. This can be very frustrating when you want the scene to have spontaneity—that is, for the children to behave naturally without any awareness of the camera. A good rule of thumb for dealing with youngsters is to set them up first in a situation that will hold their attention (keep them truly involved in the action), and then shoot the scene with a telephoto lens. Thus there is no distracting camera in the immediate vicinity, and you will be able to capture reactions that are real and spontaneous. Also, the telephoto lens will give a lovely softness to the scene—very appropriate when photographing young children.

Working with actors is no different from working with your script or your camera. Be prepared to make mistakes and even to feel a little foolish at times. But be determined also not to let these mistakes deter you from continued experimentation.

CHAPTER 7

Special Effects

Special effects can be used to point up the statement you are making in your film; they can also be a great deal of fun. Many special effects that you see in feature films are created in film laboratories. In your own filming, however, you will limit yourself to effects that you can create by using your camera in different ways—and by using your imagination.

Three of the most common effects have already been discussed: slow motion, fast motion, and reverse motion. Technically, all of them involve shooting at one speed and projecting at another.

As mentioned earlier, the rate of shooting and projection for action as we normally see it is usually twenty-four frames per second for film with sound and eighteen frames per second for 8mm and Super 8 cameras not using sound. To create an effect of slow motion in the projection of your film, you must increase the rate of speed at which you shoot. Currently, most Super 8 cameras have speeds of 12, 18, 24, 32, and more frames per second. Filming at anything faster than the normal 18 frames per second will give you the effect of slow motion. And the higher the speed of filming, the slower the motion you will achieve.

Slow motion is especially useful when you want the audience to see details of an action that could not normally be seen if shot at real speed. Thus, it is very good for bringing the fast action of sports into a form where it can be studied by the viewer: the swing of a golfer or batter or tennis player, the arm strokes and grace of a swimmer, the legs of a track runner. It is a very effective device for capturing the grace and balletic movements (if that is your intention) of a skier or pole vaulter, or when you want to give a dreamlike interpretation to your sequence. Some film makers also use slow motion when they are shooting from moving vehicles or are panning with their camera. This technique makes action look much smoother than if filmed at normal speed.

Speeded-up or fast motion is achieved by filming at much slower than normal speeds—for example, eight or twelve frames per second. Again, when projected at a normal eighteen frames per second, the action in these scenes will look faster than normal speed. Fast motion is especially good for comedy effects, partly because the audience does not have time to become emotionally involved with the actors and is therefore more objective, a basic requirement for the ability to see humor in a situation.

An important thing to remember when shooting in both slow and fast motion is that an exposure correction has to be made. In slow motion, each frame will appear behind the lens for a shorter length of time than at normal speed and so will be exposed to less light. Because of that, you will have to make your lens opening larger—usually twice as large as for normal speed. A similar problem exists when shooting in fast motion, only in reverse. Because your film will be slower, each frame will be receiving *more* light than at normal speed. Thus you will have to make your lens opening smaller—usually half the size it would be at normal speed.

Reverse motion, which is used less frequently than either fast or slow motion, can create almost magical effects. By shooting in reverse motion you can make broken pieces of glass assemble themselves into a vase, or make a burning object restore itself to its previous flameless, uncharred condition. You can make food come out from a diner's mouth uneaten, instead of going in.

You can achieve reverse motion technically in one of two

ways. First, put a cap on your lens to prevent the film from being exposed to light, and then run your film forward for whatever length you think you will need for your reverse-motion shot. After that, put your camera motor into reverse and shoot the action as you usually would. If your camera is not built to run backward, you can still shoot your scene if you hold your camera *upside down*. When you edit your film and come to the upside-down portion, simply turn it right side up. This reversal of the order of the frames causes the scene to move backward.

Another standard set of interesting effects are dissolves, fade-ins, fade-outs, and superimpositions ("supers"). Again, most of these effects are usually accomplished in the laboratory, but many cameras today have accommodations for creating them during the course of the actual shooting. When fading in, you start your camera motor on the scene, but wait a second or two before slowly opening up the shutter. For fading out at the end of a scene, you gradually close down the shutter, stop it, and then stop the camera's motor. If you rewind your footage to the point just before the last scene began to fade out, and shoot a fade-in of a new scene, you will have created the effect of a dissolve. A dissolve can be a very smooth transitional device for going from one shot or sequence to another. Dissolves can be as long as you like.

Some film makers rewind the footage far back into the previous scene and then begin shooting the next scene. The effect is startling: two scenes overlapping in the frame. This is referred to as a superimposition. With "supers" some very lovely and surreal results can be achieved as multiple images overlay each other. After much experimentation, you will be able to use this device to create fascinating, provocative sequences on film.

As mentioned before, certain movie cameras can shoot a

In a superimposition one image is laid on top of another.
Photo by Stemm

single frame at a time. One way to use this single-framing capability is in time-lapse photography, where you compress a scene that would usually take a long time into a much shorter time. The result can be most impressive.

First of all, remember that in any single-frame work it is absolutely essential that you place your camera on a tripod and keep it perfectly still between exposures. Do not move it even a hair—or your effect will be ruined. You have probably already seen time-lapse photography in film sequences showing the opening of a flower or the setting of the sun. It is generally a good idea to begin such a series of shots with two or three seconds of filming at normal speed. After that you simply expose a single frame of film at a time. The trick is to know how far apart these exposures should be. To determine that, you will have to know how long you want the sequence to run and how long the normal action of the scene you are photographing would last.

Let us say you are shooting a sunset. In reality, that action takes about an hour——but you want your sun to set in ten seconds on the screen. Divide the time of the normal action (in seconds) by the length of your movie (ten seconds). Divide the answer by the speed for normal projection (eighteen frames per second). Therefore, if you want to shoot your setting sun for a ten-second film sequence, you will shoot one frame—that is, make one exposure—every twenty seconds!

Time-lapse photography also works well for comic effects. One film maker used the technique to compress an entire football game into one minute.

A word of consolation. If your camera does not have a single-framing capability, you can still create an acceptable single-frame effect. Just flick your exposure release slightly as you shoot, and you will expose only one or two frames at a time.

A special effect that is used infrequently, but can get hilarious results, is the use of the zoom to create "jump cuts." Assume that you are going to photograph the skyline of a city. Mount your camera on a tripod, and start your zoom. Let it run for a full second, then stop it. Start it again, let it run a second, stop it. Do this several times, until you have completed the zoom into as close a shot as you can achieve. When this sequence is projected, it will seem as if the city were bouncing out at us in a series of quick zooms, like rapidly projected still photographs in which the image gets larger and larger.

Speaking of still photographs, you can use your camera for a series of still photos with one light directly on them. By zooming into them, panning across them, tilting up and down, moving across them from one image to another, you can bring them to cinematic life. Simply mount them on a wall, light them, and shoot. This technique has been frequently used with great success by documentary film makers.

One of the most enjoyable effects is making objects appear and disappear in a frame or scene. Imagine that you want one of your friends to appear suddenly on the fence around a corral. Mount your camera on a tripod and shoot the scene in which your friend is to appear. Then stop the camera, bring your friend into the frame area, and place him on the fence. Once he is positioned, return to your camera and shoot. After a few seconds, stop the camera and ask your friend to remove himself from the scene. Then start up the camera again and complete the shot as it was before your friend came into it. When this sequence is projected, your friend will appear magically on the fence, sit there for a moment or two, and then, just as magically, disappear from the scene. But remember, to achieve this effect you must not move the camera from its original position.

There are some variations on this trick. For one, with your camera on the tripod, have a child ride his bike across the frame, but stop him when he gets to the center of it—and stop the camera before he stops. Then replace his two-wheel bike with a tricycle at the point in the frame where the camera stopped filming. Put the original child on the tricycle, and shoot him as he continues moving across the frame. When this film sequence is projected, it will look as though the child has magically changed vehicles in the middle of the scene.

A myriad of special effects can be created by using a

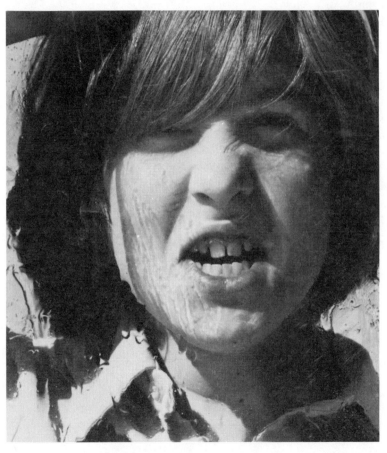

This effect was created by pouring cooking oil over a glass and then placing the glass in front of the lens.

variety of matting techniques. That means you expose only a particular portion of the film frame at one time. Professional film makers have various devices for matting, but you can get startling results by simply using pieces of black cardboard. Suppose, for example, that you were going to shoot a scene, and you wanted it to appear as though someone were looking at it through a telescope. Take a piece of black cardboard, cut a circular hole in it, and place it over your lens. When you look through your lens you will see only what the hole in the cardboard reveals to you. The camera will expose only that part of the scene that you can view through the hole.

You can use other mats for additional interesting effects. Let us say you want a friend of yours to appear to be in two places at the same time. Again, take a piece of black cardboard and mat out the right half of the frame as you shoot your friend through the left half of the frame. Then rewind the footage to the beginning of the same shot. Mat out the left half of the frame as you shoot your friend through the right half of the frame. When the shot is projected, your friend will seem to be in two places at the same time.

A variation of this effect can be done by matting out first the lower half, then the upper half of the frame (or vice versa). For example, mat out the upper half of the frame and shoot only the torso of your friend. Then rewind the footage to the beginning of the shot, mat out the lower half of the frame on your lens, and shoot the face of a large friendly dog. When your sequence is projected, the face of a dog will dangle on the body of a human being.

Many effects can be achieved by placing transparent materials in front of the lens of your camera and shooting your object through them. You can, of course, buy filters and professional devices that do the job, but this book will limit itself basically to homemade devices.

Suppose you wanted to shoot the face of a subject, but you wanted that face to look eerie and distorted. You might try filling a plate or pan with thick cooking oil and then pouring it in front of your lens while you shoot your subject. As the oil runs off the plate, the face will appear rubbery and disjointed. If you color that oil with some vegetable dye, you will create an even more bizarre effect that should be very striking on your color film.

A common trick used by many photographers is to smear a light coat of Vaseline on a piece of clear glass and then place it in front of the subject while shooting. The coating should be applied in even, circular patterns, with a small uncoated area in the center of the glass. If done properly, the effect will be one of haze and softness surrounding a sharp image in the center. Since this is a very attractive effect, it is frequently used in fashion advertisements or in TV commercials where the product or person is meant to look gentle and appealing.

If your camera can accommodate it, and if you have the money to spend, you can create similar effects with what are known as "diffusion" filters. These filters accentuate the softness and glowing highlights of a scene. They were very popular in the romantic Hollywood films of the 1930's.

Another diffusion device that has become quite popular— as a matter of fact, it has been overused—is the cross-star filter. It costs only a few dollars. When used on an object that catches highlights and reflections, it translates them into tiny stars. It, too, enhances the glamour of a scene. Its main application has been in television commercials, especially in scenes involving sun reflections on water or on glass objects such as bottles of Coke.

Given all the above possibilities for special effects, you are almost certain to come up with ideas of your own. Remember, the only way to find out how something is going to look is to try it. In the beginning, you will probably overdo

Smearing Vaseline over your lens will create this effect.

your use of special effects, mainly because you are still in the experimental stages. But later on you will find that special effects are special only if used sparingly.

CHAPTER 8

Editing

A lot of people have the notion that editing or cutting a film means getting rid of the "bad stuff." While this may describe a fraction of the editing process, it does not really explain what editing is. When you remove underexposed shots, misleading screen direction, places where your actor did not do the exact thing you had requested, or frames where a stranger accidentally walked across your shooting frame—yes, then it can be said that you are throwing out the bad stuff, getting rid of the obvious mistakes that were already apparent when you were shooting your film.

To begin really to understand the editing process, you must, as in everything else in filmmaking, do a lot of experimenting and handle a lot of film, until you begin to get the "feel" of the relationship between editing and filmic form and filmic sense. Editing really begins in the planning stages of a film project. This is why, in the beginning, your point of view is so important, and why you must determine your intention, create your plan, and adhere during the shooting process to the structure you have set for yourself.

You really start to edit the moment you decide to make a film. It is here that you already begin to accept certain ideas for your film and to reject others. If your action is going to "match" in the cutting stages, you must make certain that it matches in the shooting stages. If you are going to "intercut" shots in the editing of your film that are not obviously related (such as faces of snarling dogs with faces of angry people), you must have a pretty good idea whether it will work cinematically at the time you make your plan or treatment or shooting script.

Editing, then, is not merely something that comes last in the development of your film. It must be a way of thinking that has been going on since the very beginning. The separation of planning from camera work and camera work from editing is only a convenience. In no way can any one of these elements be fulfilled without the others. The shots you take will be determined by your scripted intention and by the editing structure you wish to give it. Conversely, your editing will be limited by what you have planned and what you have shot.

There is perhaps one exception here. You might say, "I am going to shoot an actual event that is going to take place, and I really don't know exactly what is going to happen, so I can't make a detailed plan." The answer, then, is to shoot as much as possible, if you are documenting an event such as a sports match. Get as much coverage as you can. Cover yourself with cutaways and as great a variety of different shots and different angles as is feasible. If in a project of this kind you can get a friend to operate a second camera while you are busy with the first, by all means do so.

When you edit your film, chances are that you will be working directly with the processed film, and after being edited it will be directly projected to your audiences.

Professional film makers do not work directly with their original materials or footage. After a professional film has been shot, the exposed film will be either in reversal or negative. This original material is first taken to a laboratory to be processed, and then what is called a "work print" is made from it. A work print is an untimed positive print of the original material or film, an exact duplicate of everything that has been shot.

The advantage of a work print is that the editor can work on it for a long time—changing shots in sequences, cutting them down, altering them, pulling splices apart, making new splices—without damaging the original film.

This original, after the work print is made, is kept in the film laboratory in a dry, dust-free vault. Only after the work print has been cut is the original cut. Using the work print as a model, the "matcher" cuts the original to correspond exactly to the cut work print. Then, from the final matched original, the eventual composite prints are made. They are the prints that are projected in one continuous strand with no visible splices or editorial markings.

Professional editing is generally done on a machine called

Moviola—vertical editing
Courtesy Magnasync Moviola Corporation

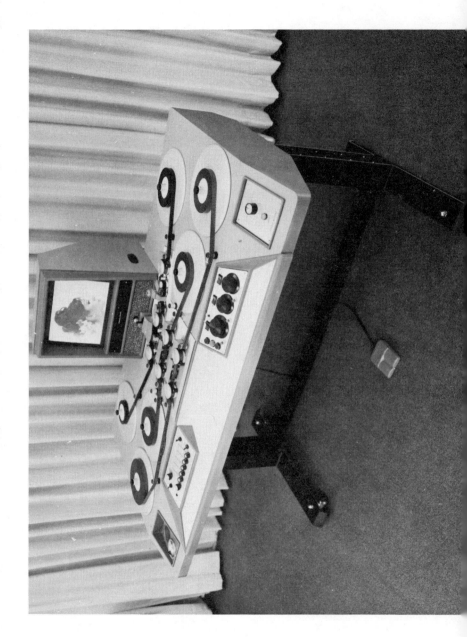

a Moviola, where the cutting is done vertically. Recently, however, there has been increased use of another kind of machine, the Steenbeck, which permits the professional film maker to work with his film horizontally. The latter has become increasingly popular because its mechanisms are very easy on the work print—that is, there is less tendency for sprocket holes to be torn or for the picture to be ripped—and editing can be done in less time than on the machines using the older vertical method of cutting. Moviola has recently developed its own horizontal editing table.

Both the Moviola and the Steenbeck have a picture-viewing head and a magnetic-sound head. Sound and picture heads are linked together so that they can be run together in sync, frame by frame. This is very important when you are cutting a sync-sound film or segment. The sound and picture tracks can also be run separately, independently of each other. Both machines can also be stopped on any single frame of film, then run backward or forward at any number of desired speeds. These machines permit the professional editor to cut sync footage or silent footage, or to combine both. Occasionally the film maker without too many financial or technical resources will cut his film by using only a viewer in combination with a device called a synchronizer.

To edit your 8mm or Super 8 films technically, you will need a viewer, a pair of rewinds, a splicer, and splicing tape. If you do not have a viewer, you can use your projector. Some companies manufacture an entire editor-viewer-splicer machine. You might look into the versatile Craig Editor Model KE-Super 8 or Model KE-8, or the Honeywell Elmo Dual Editor (for 8mm) or Super 8 (for Super 8 and Single 8 film). The Craig machine has a comparatively large viewing

Moviola—horizontal editing

Courtesy Magnasync Moviola Corporation

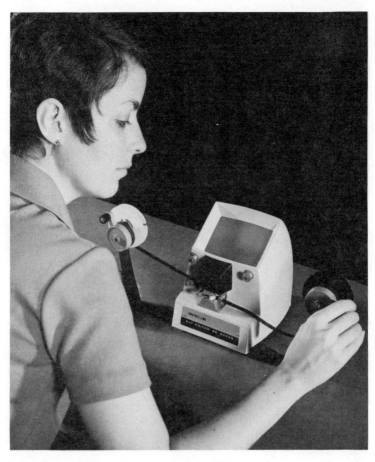

The Honeywell Elmo 8mm SE (Super Editor)
Courtesy Carl Byoir & Associates, Inc.
Honeywell Photographic Products Division

screen, straddled by a pair of rewinds on both sides. It has a built-in frame marker, which identifies frames for cutting and removal; a splicer that permits splicing by tape or cement; and a simple-to-operate focusing adjustment that provides clear, sharp pictures of your footage. The Honeywell-Elmo Dual and Super Editors also have large viewing screens,

frame markers for identifying the frames you wish to eliminate, and a capacity for still projection that lets you view
the film frame by frame by turning the viewing knob.

If you cannot afford a viewer-editor, you will need at
least a splicer. Two of the best are the Eumig Chemo Splicer
Z01 or Z02 (for Super 8 and 8mm, respectively) and the Guillotine 8mm Splicer manufactured by the Guillotine Splicer
Corporation. The Eumig splicer makes a true butt splice,
and eliminates overlap and scraping. The serrated edges of
the splicer are cut into the film ends and interlock them
to form a butt splice.

Guillotine has produced professional splicers for many
years, and has recently made a precision 8mm splicing fa-
cility. The Guillotine splicer operates without cement, heat,
or splice tabs. The film is held firmly on the splicer by ten
registration pins and a full-length pressure plate. Mylar tape
is then pulled across the film at a right angle to the line of
the film, which means that no tape-to-film alignment is required. You simply smooth the tape down on the film. Then
you press down the perforator lever and punch three perfectly film-registered sprocket holes into the applied tape,
simultaneously cutting it to the film width. After that, you
just fold the measured tape tab to the other side of the film
to complete the splice. The Guillotine splicer is also excellent
for repairing torn film and broken sprocket holes. Most
other machines work the same way—with slight variations.

The difference between the splicing of professional films
and what you will be doing is the "work-print" step mentioned earlier. The professional film editor will generally
make *tape* splices on his work print. However, when this
work print is taken to the "matcher," and the original material is cut to it, the original material is spliced together
with hot cement splices. Tape splices offer the advantage of
not being permanent. You can peel off the tape from the
splice and readjust the shot or sequence as many times as
necessary. This is extremely important if you are to have the

creative latitude for experimentation that you need in editing. A cement splice, on the other hand, *is* permanent; the only way you can change a cut under these circumstances is to cut out the splice. When you do that, you lose one frame of picture on each side of the splice line. A loss of one or two frames can throw a professional "sync" sequence completely out of sync. The cement splice, however, is the only method used for working with the original material, not only because it is permanent but also because a tape splice would cause a visible disturbance for several frames on each side of the cut over which it is laid.

Most likely, then, you will be doing tape splicing with your 8mm and Super 8 films, and most of these splicers require essentially the same procedure:

1. Place the film to be spliced on the registration pins.
2. Apply the pressure-sensitive tape to each side of the film where you made the cuts.

When working with your film, try to keep it as scratch-free as possible. It is wise to invest in a pair or pairs (they are very inexpensive) of editing gloves (thin white-cotton gloves) and wear them at all times during your editing. When you have completed your editing, and are satisfied that what you have created is to be your permanent film, "clean" your footage. This can be done with Kodak Movie Film Cleaner, which removes dirt and fingerprints. At the same time it lubricates your film for steady projection.

Editing, therefore, does not mean just throwing out the bad stuff. Your editing begins the moment you begin to think about your film and your intention with it. Remember, you will only be able to work in your editing with those materials that you have had the foresight to gather in your shooting. This does not mean, of course, that if you view all of your footage and feel you need some more shots to bring your film to cinematic life, you should not abandon the editing for a while and go out and get those shots.

After you have brought all your footage back from shooting, it is wise to make a log or an inventory of exactly how much and what kind of footage you have. First of all, look at all of it many times in the viewer until you know it by heart and can almost cut the film in your head. Think about your footage and juxtapose various shots and scenes in your mind (that inexpensive projector that runs in your head is one of your most valuable filmmaking tools).

Since you will have much more processed film than you will actually be using in your completed work, it is a good idea to break it down. If there are five scenes in your film script, you must first separate your footage into the specific five scenes. Get a memo pad or some index cards and head each one with a working title for each scene, for instance, Snow Scene, Beach Scene, Forest Scene, etc. Once the film has been divided into the five specific scenes, you will be able to break it down into further sequences and then into specific shots. Let's assume you have your five scenes listed on cards. One of these scenes you have titled "Beach Scene." Under the Beach Scene you will put various sequences and shots:

C. Beach Scene
   1. Girl playing with dog on beach
       a. Close-up of dog
       b. Medium shot of girl and dog
       c. Long shot of girl and dog with ocean behind

   2. Pan with old man walking across beach, frame left to right
       a. Medium shot of man walking toward lens, head-on
       b. Reverse angle of man walking away from lens

   3. Long shot of deserted beach, head-on, waves coming toward lens

    a. Medium shot of deserted beach, waves coming toward lens
    b. High-angle shot of waves on sand, tide going in and out
    c. Close-ups (2) footprints in the sand

4. Gulls
    a. Long shot of several gulls on beach
    b. Medium shot of single gull flying, camera moving with him
    c. Pan with bird walking across frame, left to right

5. Two boys playing ball on beach
    a. Long shot
    b. Medium shot of one boy throwing ball, shot from over shoulder of other boy, ball moving toward camera
    c. Close-up of boy catching ball
    d. Cutaway close-up of boy's feet running on sand

Although your list might be longer or shorter, this is the general idea of a scene breakdown. When you go through your footage, you will make a more detailed list on which you will include those shots that you felt were not successful and that—even at this point—you are pretty certain you will not want to use in your film. This breakdown will let you know immediately what is available to you and on which film roll you have put it. You will also be able to do much of your cutting by referring to these cards first, then trying out your decisions on the viewer or projector after splicing. In addition, after you have broken down your footage and noted it on the cards, you might try revising your script or plan according to your card list and then editing your film by following the revised script.

After the breakdown, and before you have begun splicing, it is a good idea to arrange your shots in such a way that you will have ready access to them. For example, you can

NOW IT'S EASY TO MAKE TIGHT, NOISE-FREE SPLICES...

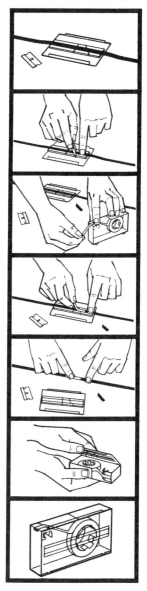

1 Place tape within splicing block guide channel, *backing side up.* Overlap ends. (Tip: Fold back end of top piece of tape and crease, for easy removal after cutting.)

2 Hold tape firmly in channel with finger and cut with sharp, demagnetized razor blade (45° diagonal cut for regular splices, 90° cut for editing splices).

3 Pull out approximately 1 inch of splicing tape and draw downward against cutting blade . . . use finger to hold tape on dispenser platform to prevent slippage, for cleanest cut.

4 Keep tape ends butted tightly together and lay splicing tape carefully on top, inside channel. Press down lightly to adhere tape full length of splice.

5 Remove spliced tape from channel and rub splicing tape firmly with fingernail to remove all air bubbles. Now you have a lifetime splice!

6 Clip splicing block to open side of dispenser for convenient kit storage. Keep in a clean, dry place when not in use. (If splicing tape isn't used for several weeks, remove length that has been exposed to air before next splicing use, to assure fresh, clean adhesive contact.)

Courtesy Magnetic Products Division, 3M Company, St. Paul, Minn.

hang the strips of film (labeled with a piece of tape at the end) on a bulletin board by inserting push pins into the sprocket holes.

Now you are ready to splice your shots into the desired order. Remember, in splicing you will be attaching the beginning of one shot to the end of another. If you do not do that, some of your scenes will come out upside down when projected in a projector or viewer.

As you continue to make movies, you will find that more and more of your editing will occur in camera because, mentally, you are developing a filmic sense and are learning gradually how to translate that into film form.

It is important while editing to keep in mind the rule about matching action from long shot to medium shot to close-up. Often you will discover that although you thought you had carefully matched the action while you were shooting, the shots do not blend smoothly when put together. You have a boy in a restaurant, for example. He takes a drink of water. You have a long shot of him reaching for the glass, and then putting it to his lips. You have a medium shot of him picking up the glass, putting it to his lips, and drinking the water. When you cut this sequence and want to go from LS to MS, you will have to be careful to trim your shots. Otherwise, when you go to the second shot, it will look as though the boy is again reaching for the same glass that he reached for in the long shot. To match the action smoothly, you will have to pick up the movement at the exact point in the second shot where you left off in the first shot.

Another thing to remember in your editing (as well as in your planning and shooting) is the unique capacity of film both to compress and to expand time. You can easily shrink an action that would normally take several minutes or even more into a few seconds on the screen—and your audience will accept it as "real." How many times, for example, have you seen a character in a feature film say that he was going to catch the next plane to London, and then watched as his remark was followed by a plane taking off and then landing at an airport (appropriately identified with a sign). In reality, the trip would have taken hours. But on the motion-picture screen, the audience readily accepts its duration of only several seconds. The plane landing is our visual clue that our character has arrived in London safely.

In editing, screen time can often be compressed with the use of cutaways. You want to show your class entering school, sitting in the classroom, and leaving after the day is over. You shoot them going into the school, take a variety of shots of them in the classroom, and then take more shots as they depart. Also, you shoot a cutaway of the school clock about to mark the hour of dismissal time. Enhanced by the sound of a school bell on the film's track, this cutaway— inserted between the shots in the classroom and the children leaving the school—will help tell a long story in several seconds.

The major point to remember about such a cutaway is that it should be different enough in viewpoint or subject matter from the main action for the references of time and place in the main action to be dropped temporarily and then be resumed without any awkwardness.

Expanding action in a film is very often deliberately used to create suspense. Let's return to our earlier example of the bicycle race. The race itself might have lasted only thirty seconds in reality, but in shooting you wanted to make the audience experience a sense of apprehension as to who the winner would be. You took a variety of shots from a variety of angles. When you edited them, you inserted at least half a dozen shots of close-ups of the faces of the two participants, constantly intercutting between the two. The screen time for the actual thirty-second event was a minute. By expanding the event beyond its real proportions of time and space, you were able to create suspense as to its outcome and certainly give more vitality to the sequence.

Finally, although you will not be getting into too much of this in your early stages as a film maker, it should be pointed out that the process of editing—the juxtaposing of one shot next to another—can help the film attain rather remarkable levels of intellectual and emotional impact on the motion-picture screen. To begin to understand this, forget for a moment the tasks of matching screen direction, creating smooth continuity, matching action from long shot to close-up. Think about what happens when you put two seemingly unrelated subjects or shots together.

Let us say that the audience first sees a shot of a boy. It sees a close-up of his face. Then there is a shot of a nice big bowl of spaghetti. Almost automatically the audience will relate the spaghetti to the boy. If his face is unhappy, the audience will probably assume that he is also very hungry and has not had a dish of spaghetti in a long time. If he is smiling, the audience will probably assume that he sees the bowl of spaghetti and is about to devour it. Thus, you had one image (boy) next to another image (bowl of spaghetti), and the combination created a *third* image in the mind of the audience (the boy was hungry or he was going to eat the spaghetti). Here you have an example—rudimentary though it might be—of something upon which the modern cinema has been based since the days of Sergei Eisenstein (its creator): *intellectual montage.* Two images placed next to each other create a third image in the mind of the audience. Film makers have used this editing concept thousands of times to clarify their thematic or emotional intention for the audience.

Another example would be a shot of a man in prison, staring from a barred window. Next, we see a bird taking off from the roof of an institutional building. With these two images confronting the audience, one after the other, chances are that they will be moved to feel a sense of the prisoner's frustration—he, too, would like to be as free as that bird, liberated from his situation in life.

This same concept can be used to create visual "tricks." For example, if we see a shot of a boy staring up at the sky— a close-up that does not reveal exactly what the child is looking at—and then this shot is followed by a low-angle shot of the Empire State Building, the audience will again join the two shots in their mind. They will assume that the boy is staring up at the Empire State Building (even though child and building might, in reality, be separated by thousands of miles).

A classic example of this kind of editing trick is the following: The first shot shows a child in profile looking toward the left of the frame. The second shot is of the Capitol dome in Washington, D.C. The third shot is of the same child now looking in profile toward the right of the frame. The final shot is of the Kremlin in Moscow. The effect of this sequence in the mind of the audience is that when the child looks to the left, he sees Washington, and when he looks to the right, he sees Moscow. Absurd? Absolutely, but this is the magical potential that the art of editing and our sense of film form offer us. It is up to us to use it in ways that are more than mere illustrative tricks, ways that will make our films more meaningful to ourselves and to our audiences.

CHAPTER 9

Sound for Your Film

Adding sound to your films will make them much more
appealing to your audience, and you will find that the element of sound is another way to express your filmic intention. Chances are you will be limited technically, but that
should not hinder you from exploring the full dimensions
of what is available to you in sound.

You have probably seen many features in which "sync"
sound was used—that is, the sounds of the actors' speech
synchronized with their lip movements on the screen. But
you may be surprised to learn that even in sync-sound features rarely more than half the film is actually recorded or
shot in sync. Most of the time it is scattered through the film
intermittently, and is enhanced by silent footage covered
with sound effects and music and "voice-over" sound—that
is, dialogue without discernible lip movements that is heard
"over" the scene. In addition, many dialogue scenes are
recorded for voice during a "post-dubbing" process in a recording studio, after the sequence itself has been shot without sync sound. The actors watch the sequence as it is
projected on a screen in a studio, then match their voices
and expressions to the lip movements of the actors on the
screen.

In recording professional sync sound, there are several options open to the film maker. First of all, he will use different
microphones, depending on the kind of situation that is to
be filmed. If he is shooting an intimate sync-sound scene of
two people in quiet conversation, he will want to achieve

as much presence in the ultimate results as he possibly can. "Presence" means that the voices of the actors will sound very close to the ears of the listeners or viewers rather than coming from a distance. For this, the film maker will most likely use a "directional" microphone. This is very sensitive to sounds directly in front of it and insensitive to sounds from a distance, thus not picking up much background noise. The mike would be connected to a cable or wire, which would be connected to the sync-sound tape recorder.

Now, if the same two actors decided to continue their conversation while walking, the film maker might readily use that same mike, but it would be suspended over the actors' heads. The mike would also be mounted on the end of a pole ("fishpole") carried by a sound assistant who would walk along with the two actors, but stay out of the frame of the film. The audience would see only the actors. The mike, the "fishpole," and the assistant sound man would be out of view.

If that same film maker were shooting a sync-sound segment that involved two actors speaking to each other from a distance, he might use two small mikes hung around the necks of the actors and concealed in part of their clothing. These small mikes are called lavalier mikes, and they are becoming increasingly popular. You may, in fact, have seen them on TV interview or talk shows. Lavalier mikes have a cable running from them, and since more than one mike is used, the cables are not run directly into the tape recorder, but go first into a "mixer." The mixer allows the sound man, during the process of sync-sound filming, to adjust the actors' voices to a desirable medium level, which is then fed into the recorder. It is very important that the sound man wear earphones while recording so he can listen to the sound being recorded and "monitor" it. There may be distracting, undesirable noises in the scene occasionally, which will not be heard by the director or cameraman but will be picked up by the tape recorder.

There are several good sound cameras for shooting sync scenes. What is required, in addition to the tape recorder and cables, is a camera that is capable of running, without any variation, at sound speed—that is, 24 frames per second. The tape recorder generally used is a Nagra ¼-inch tape recorder, which has a timing reference that synchronizes picture to sound. Synchronous sound can be shot with the tape recorder connected directly to the camera by a cable, or it can be shot without any mechanical connection at all between tape recorder and camera. This latter method is referred to as "crystal sync." It requires a camera and tape recorder with timing standards that operate at the same frequency. The advantage of shooting crystal sync is that the cameraman is able to move independently of the sound man, thus giving the film maker much more physical freedom.

Shooting professional sync sound also requires two other major items. First of all, many cameras make noise as the film motor advances the film. To avoid this, you must use a camera that is virtually noise-free. Or, if that is not available, you must "blimp" the camera. A "blimp" is a device placed on a camera that insulates or soundproofs it. If these precautions are not taken, chances are that the recorder will pick up the noise of the running camera. Also, in shooting sync sound, the visuals the camera takes will later, in the editing process, have to be lined up *exactly* with the dialogue that the tape recorder registers. If that is not done, the lip movements of the actors will be out of sync with the recorded dialogue.

To ensure exact sync, "slating" is used. This means that after the camera and the tape recorder have started rolling, a small slate, with the scene number and other information written on it, is placed in front of the camera lens. On top of this slate is a stick that is fastened to it at one end with a hinge. The assistant doing the slating claps this stick down on top of the slate. Later the editor will line up this clapping sound with the point on the developed film where the stick comes down on the slate. Thus he ensures that the sound and picture are together, or in sync.

For your own sync-sound shooting, there are a few options. One is the Bell and Howell Filmosound 8 system, which consists of a camera, a cassette tape recorder, and a projector. The camera uses Super 8 cartridge film, and the recorder uses conventional cassette tape cartridges. The camera and tape recorder are portable, and the recorder has a shoulder strap that allows you to use both hands to operate the camera. The synchronized tape recorder plugs into the camera and automatically starts recording as you start to shoot a subject or scene. Whether it is dialogue or sound effects, it is matched to each frame of film. To play your sequence or film with sound, you merely plug the tape recorder into the projector and play both simultaneously. The sound on the tape will come out matched to the movements on the screen. In addition, if you choose, you can have your cassette tape transferred onto a magnetic strip of sound that is placed permanently on the film itself. This will eliminate using the tape recorder every time you want to project your sound film.

Without this or a similar system, you will still be able to create at least the illusion of sync sound. For example, you want to shoot a group of children having a conversation in a park. Perhaps they are having a picnic, sitting on the ground, eating, and chatting. You might place your tape recorder and mike very close to them—close enough so that you will not pick up too many extraneous noises—and conceal the recorder behind the picnic basket or some foliage. Then, as the recorder registers their conversation, you shoot the scene from a distance with your telephoto lens. This way, you will certainly not pick up any camera noise on your tape recorder.

You might also record "voice over" conversations or dialogue. Let us say you shoot two children playing on a beach at sunset. You shoot them from a distance and at such angles that the audience cannot see their lip movements. Then you put aside your camera, move up to them with your tape recorder, and record their conversations and their laughter "wild"—that is, nonsync. When the sequence is cut and projected, your audience will see the children on the beach and hear their conversation with great "presence." They will not worry at all about nonsynchronized lip movements. This same approach has been used in countless feature films.

"Wild sound" can be very important in adding reality to your films. Even when you are shooting a silent scene, it is advisable to have a tape recorder handy to pick up any sound effects that you think you might want to use in the film. When doing wild sound outdoors, you will need a battery-powered tape recorder, preferably one that is portable. Suppose you were back at the beach with the children playing. It would be a good idea to record the sound of the surf and the sea gulls so you could cut them into your film later on.

Whenever you are recording, remember to play back each sound effect or sequence after you have taped it. Unless you have a pair of earphones and an excellent monitoring device on your tape recorder, you will have no idea whether you have done your recording at the desired level. Also, without playing it back immediately, you will not know whether your microphone has picked up any unwanted noises. A typical example of this is wind. To the human ear, wind sounds gentle and unobtrusive. On the mike, wind creates a distorting, booming effect that will turn what should be a quiet scene on the beach into a noisy, cluttered segment predominantly of static. Do not let your ears deceive you. Play back your recording immediately, or you might find yourself having to make another trip to the same location.

You can very quickly build up your own library of sound effects if you use your tape recorder frequently. On some occasions, however, you might want effects that you cannot record by yourself. For example, you may be shooting a comedy sequence in which one of your friends gets angry and starts throwing tomatoes at another friend. On the film's track, you may want the sounds of bombs going off. Rest assured. There are plenty of sound-effects records available, and they can be purchased inexpensively, especially since you are doing a noncommercial production. In addition to sounds of real things, there are sound-effects records that have specially created sounds, such as bizarre electronic noises. Do not ever feel limited. You can purchase a sound effect of almost anything you will ever want—and if it is so unique that it is not available, then try making it yourself with some ingenuity and experimentation.

In addition to dialogue or narration or sound effects for your track, it might also be desirable to consider the possibilities that music offers. Music is ideal for relaxing your viewers, and is particularly useful for creating a certain emotional feeling or mood. There are many commercial supply houses that have film music for sale, usually short pieces that have been created especially to evoke a particular background mood. Of course, since you are not as yet making commercial films, you have your own record collection to draw from, or even the radio.

If you have a friend or group of friends who play instruments, you might even be able to have an original score for your film.

One of the best ways to proceed is to let your musician friends take a look at your film and then improvise a few selections against the action on the screen. Both you and they will be able to tell what is going to work most effectively. And after you have decided, you will simply set up a recording session in as quiet a place as possible. Since you will not have access to a professional recording studio, you might have to make some alterations on the quiet corner in which you do decide to do the live recording. For ex-

ample, it is good to have a place that is as "dead" as possible
—that is, where the sound does not have a tendency to
reverberate or "boom." One way to deaden a room is by
putting as many blankets as you can on the floor and walls.

When you consider the music for your film, you will have
to decide what you want your audience to experience. You
do not have to take the first choice that comes to mind or
seems the most workable. For example, if you have lively
action, you will probably want to enhance it with lively music.
Conversely, if your action is slow, you might choose slow
music. But remember that pace or rhythm is not the sole
thing to consider in your selection. If you think strictly in
these terms, you will limit yourself severely—and miss out
on a great deal of fun and satisfaction as well.

In thinking of music, you must again think of your intention. Suppose you shot sequences at the zoo, animals of all
varieties in the process of cleaning themselves. You would
point up the humor of your footage if you cut the scene to
the beat of a very sophisticated, fully orchestrated tango.
Still remaining with the example of the zoo, let us say that
you shot a series of animals walking. The hippopotamus
might walk to the accompaniment of parade drums; the
flamingo might move to the sound of a fiddle or banjo; the
penguins might waddle to the sound of flutes.

Occasionally you might substitute music for sound effects.
We see someone running on screen in a suspense movie. But
instead of hearing his feet moving, we hear the sound of
steady, throbbing string instruments. A single bird in flight
might be accompanied on the track by a symphonic cre-
scendo—assuming the statement you want to make about
the bird and the flight is that it is a thing of beauty and gran-
deur. If you have a sequence showing a person crying, music
might conceivably alter the entire effect of the character's emotional state on the audience. By your musical choice, you can
poke fun at the crying and therefore at the character (a muted
trumpet blows some dissonant notes), or you can heighten

the audience's empathy for it (a soft gentle violin). Music is one of the most versatile of all our cinematic tools, and often the best musical choices are not always the most obvious ones.

Tape recorders run at various speeds. You will be doing your recording either on a reel-to-reel recorder or on a cassette tape recorder. Almost all cassette tape recorders record at 1⅞ inches per second; reel-to-reel recorders usually record at 3¾ inches per second (or "ips") or at 7½ ips. Some recorders also record at 15 ips, which is generally considered the ideal speed for recording music professionally.

If you are using a cassette recorder, it is best that you use Scotch high-energy recording tapes, which can be purchased in cassettes having thirty, forty-five, sixty, or ninety minutes per side. The most commonly used is the sixty-minute cassette. If you are using a reel-to-reel recorder, Scotch Open Reel Tape #207 is good because it has a high output and very low noise. You can get forty-five minutes on each side of a seven-inch reel of tape, recording at a speed of 7½ ips. If you record at a speed of 3¾ ips, you will be able to get ninety minutes on each side.

If you need a lot of time to record and do not want to change tapes frequently, it is advisable to use the 3¾ ips recording speed. But also keep in mind that running at slower speeds makes the cutting of the tape more difficult, because the tape is, in effect, more crowded. This is why most professional sound recording—at least of effects and voices—is done at 7½ ips. It is advisable that you record at the same speed on your reel-to-reel recorder.

You can use variable recording speeds to create special sound effects. For example, if you record at 3¾ ips and play back that recording at 7½ ips, the human voice will sound speeded up, which might be very effective over a humorous phone conversation in the visuals. Conversely, if you record at 7½ and play back at 3¾, the effects or voices will sound very slowed down. Again, you might use this for a deliberate effect. Remember, however, that since most of your recording will be done at 7½ ips, you will have to dub anything that you played back (for deliberate effect) at 3¾ ips—that is, you will have to transfer that exact effect to the regular 7½ ips speed. To do this, you simply play the first effect at 3¾ ips on one tape machine while simultaneously re-recording it onto another machine running at the proper speed of 7½ ips. That allows you to splice your special effect into any ¼-inch track that has been recorded at 7½ ips. Naturally, you do not have to go through the dubbing procedure if you recorded something at 3¾ ips with the intent of playing it at 7½ ips for the special effect. You just add it to your regular track.

In professional work, after the recording is done on ¼-inch tape (narration, sound effects, music, sync dialogue, etc.), you must go through another process before cutting sound to picture. All of the ¼-inch tape must first be fed into a machine called a "resolver," which "transfers" the ¼-inch magnetic tape onto ¼-inch magnetic film. Whether it is 16mm or 35mm, this magnetic film has sprocket holes on both sides, and it puts the sound in the same physical medium as the picture. That means that the editor can work simultaneously on both film and sound in frame-to-frame synchronization.

Chances are that you will not go through the process of transferring your ¼-inch tapes into magnetic tracks. Instead, you will do all of your sound editing with the ¼-inch tapes themselves. Say you have made a three-minute film about the city, emphasizing crowds and faces. You have three sound elements: voice narration, sound effects, and music. The voice narration consists of interviews with several people who talk about the city. You have twenty minutes of tape, and you have already decided—by working with your picture—that you will need only a minute and a half of those voice-over interviews for your three-minute film. You have worked with the tape machine already, and you know exactly what lines you want to use and at what points in the film you will use them. You are now going to cut a voice track for your film.

First of all, you will have to splice your original tape. Because you have recorded at 7½ ips, you have much more free space to work with and consequently less chance of snipping off something that you wanted to keep. Just put your entire tape on your tape recorder and splice out the unwanted parts.

Tape is spliced by overlapping two ends of the tape, then cutting them diagonally. It is important to make this diagonal cut, because it minimizes the noise as the splice goes through the playback head of the tape machine. Then take both ends of the parts you wish to keep and place them on the table or on a splicing device with the uncoated side up. Align the two ends, and join them together with a piece of Scotch splicing tape, applying it firmly to ensure that the splice is tight. Then simply trim off any excess splicing tape with a scissors. Proceed to the next cut you wish to make and go through the same process again. Continue in this way until you have only those sound passages that you want to keep.

Since your sound track is now only a minute and a half long, and your film is three minutes long, you will have to place either blank tape or tape leader between the sections until you have created a tape that is as long as your film. For example, you may not want the first voice to be heard until thirty seconds into the film. Therefore, you will place thirty seconds' worth of blank leader in front of your first voice. Then you will splice it (in the same way) to your first voice. If your second voice does not come for ten seconds after the first voice, you will splice in blank tape leader (ten seconds' worth) after your first voice. Do this until you have a voice track that is as long as your film.

Follow this same procedure for your music and effects track (your M & E track, as it is called). But remember, you can only do that if you are confining your sound effects to those blank spaces in which you have no music. Even though

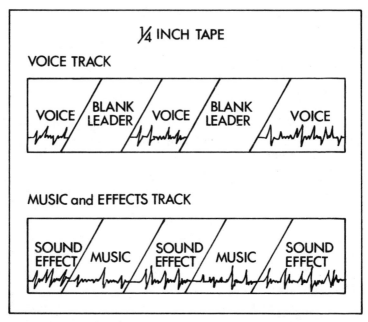

Lining up two tracks

the music runs only two minutes total (although it runs intermittently), your track will, again, be as long as your picture. Cut the music track first, filling in the "blank spaces" with tape leader. Then, into this track, splice the sound effects wherever you want them. For example, you have fifteen seconds of music, then five seconds of traffic noises, then twenty seconds of music, then ten seconds of traffic noises or whatever. Now you have a music-and-effects track together with a voice track.

A cut picture can have any number of sound tracks before they are all blended into one. Professional film makers usually use a professional "mixing" studio to mix many tracks into one. In the mixing session all the tracks are recorded in combination on a single strand of magnetic track. In the studio there are a large number of magnetic-film playback machines to accommodate the separate sound tracks that the film maker may bring in. Each of these playback decks feeds into a master control panel operated by a professional engineer, and each panel has a separate volume control. During the mixing session, they all run in sync, frame for frame, while the picture is projected. The engineer or mixer blends the tracks together, perhaps fading in the music when the voice is fading out, or suddenly "bumping up" a sound effect and then fading it out for the music to come in. He equalizes, stabilizes all the tracks into one, so that the finished sound is a mixture of finely orchestrated elements in perfect balance.

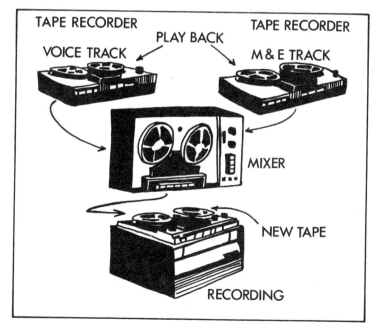

Doing your own mixing

After the professional mixing is completed, the magnetic sound track that results is then transferred to what we call an "optical" sound track. This puts the sound track into photographic form so it can be printed on the film itself whenever the "composite" print is made.

You, of course, will not have access to a professional sound-mixing studio, but you might consider mixing your own ¼-inch tracks. Since you have two tracks for the film you are making on the city, you will need, in order to mix them into one track, three tape recorders, a volume-control mixer, and cables to hook all the equipment together. The two tracks are put on separate tape recorders. On the third tape recorder, you would place a roll of new ("virgin") tape. Start the third tape recorder first, and then the two with the finished tracks on them. These tracks would ultimately be fed into the third recorder and onto the new tape. You have made your own mix!

If you do not own a tape recorder and cannot borrow one, you still might add a sound dimension to your silent footage by reading a narration over it that you have prepared in advance, or by playing a record that you have selected because of the vitality that it adds to your film.

In order to have sound, it is not necessary to use your tape recorder every time you show your film. If you have a Super 8 sound projector, you can take your mixed ¼-inch track and have it transferred automatically into what is called a "magnetic sound strip." This is then applied to the edge of your processed film. Kodak has a Sonotrack Coating Service, and in most cases you can make provisions for sound striping your film at your film dealer's. Then, every time you show your film on the sound projector, the relationship between picture and sound will always be the same.

CHAPTER 10

Animation You Can Do

When you think of animated films, the first thing that comes to mind is probably cartoons. That is not surprising, because for years professional animators have delighted us all with the antics of fantasy characters, made almost lifelike through the special techniques of animation.

But the cartoon is only one in a wide range of possibilities for using the technique of animation. Any object that moves or is movable can be animated, and you can do it with the simplest of equipment and a little imagination. In fact, this is the one technique in filmmaking that lets you create almost any situation or effect or character that you can think of.

Up to this point, we have been talking about "live-action" films. This term simply means that the camera records what is happening within the limits of reality—i.e., we see in a shot a reproduction of an event in the same time and space contexts as we would if we were watching it in reality. We might see a boy running across a field. He comes to a six-foot-high fence, and we watch him climb the fence and drop to the other side. His action seems real to us. There is nothing unusual about a boy climbing a fence. But suppose when the boy reached the fence he sprang over it in a single leap. This is an impossible situation, created through the technique of animation. Our boy is no longer an average one. He is a "superboy" who can perform any action you can imagine.

Very simply, then, animation is a technique that allows you to make things happen that could not happen in real life, and to give life to objects that have no real life of their own.

There are many, many methods of animation, and most of them can be done very simply with little equipment. You will find that this technique is not really difficult to learn. Once you have experimented with some easy exercises so that you understand the principles, you will be able to film your wildest ideas in a simple and effective way.

You can begin with nothing more than a fine-tipped felt pen and pieces of 16mm clear leader, which you can get free from any professional film producer or film laboratory. It is best to use 16mm leader for this exercise, because it will give you a wider surface to draw upon. You can make up a story and draw it on the leader, developing the action frame by frame as you go. You can also use just a series of shapes and colors to create a feeling or mood, much as you might do an abstract painting. Try using different-colored pens, making the colors run together in some frames and using them alone in others. Let the ink dry and then project this strip of film.

On a fresh strip of film, experiment with shapes—circles, dots, triangles. Find out what happens when you use the same shape in the same position in the frame for five or six frames, then draw it larger in the next five or six frames. When you get an effect you like, try projecting your strips of film with music and sound effects played on a tape recorder or a record player.

Now try another exercise. Choose a shape and a color—let us say a small circle in red. Decide on a movement for this circle across the frame. Draw the movement frame by frame. In order to know how long this movement will last, mark off your leader every 24 frames (one second of screen time). If you want your movement to last two seconds, you must make it happen in 48 frames; if three seconds, 72 frames.

Perhaps you want your circle to go back where it started (see Illustration A). Once you have made your first movement, you can continue with new movements and add different moving parts to the frame (see Illustration B). Project

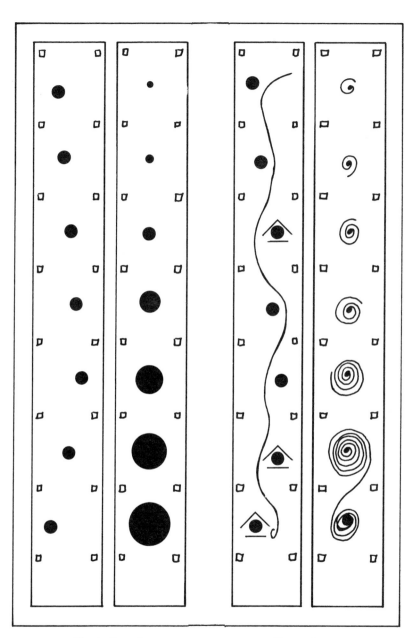

Illustration A   Illustration B

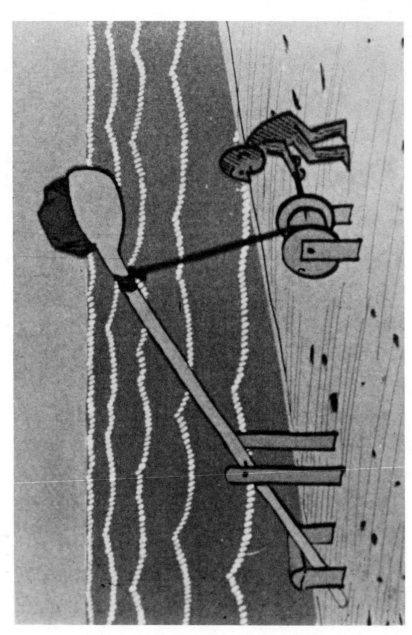

The Animated Film: Courtesy Contemporary Films/McGraw-Hill

The Animated Film:
Parcels

your film with each new addition. Keep in mind the number of frames you use for a move and the screen time each movement takes. This exercise will give you a good sense of the principle of time in animation.

Once you have completed the experiments with clear leader, you might want to try something similar with 16mm black leader. With a stylus scratch shapes and lines on each frame on the emulsion side of the leader. (Be careful not to scratch through the base of the film or it will tear in the projector.) Follow the same steps you did with the clear leader and see what kind of effect you get.

When you are ready to try animation techniques with your camera, remember that although it is not a very difficult process, it is a very time-consuming one that requires patience and *very careful planning.* As you know, a movie is a series of still pictures, each of which shows a small piece of the action photographed. When projected at a standard speed, let us say 18 frames per second, you have the impression of movement. What you are really seeing, in one second, is 18 different still photographs. In shooting live action, the photographer exposes each individual frame of his film in sequence, at the speed at which it is to be projected. The movement on the screen is an exact representation of the movement of an object or person in real time and space. In shooting animation, each frame is exposed one at a time and the photographer must chart each movement in a series of individual frames. Animated film, then, is a series of still photographs just as live action is, but in this case the photographer constructs the movement of the image rather than simply recording natural movement. When you animate, you alter time and space.

The most important piece of equipment required to shoot animation is a camera with a single-framing device that lets you shoot one frame at a time. For best results, the camera should allow you to adjust the exposure for each frame as you shoot it. If the exposures are even, you will get a smooth movement with no change in the background from frame to frame. If the exposures change, even slightly, from frame to frame, you will get a jerky or fluttering effect when you project the picture. Also, with adjustable exposures, the possibility exists of changing exposure on purpose to create effects.

It is absolutely necessary that your camera be mounted on a very steady tripod or on an animation stand. One of the principles of animation is that, although the camera is free to move forward and backward from the picture, generally it should not move north, south, east, or west. There is one exception to this rule: the technique of photomation. In this technique the camera is free to cover all areas of a photograph in whatever way the photographer chooses, but the parts of the photograph remain still. In standard animation, even a slight change of camera position in a horizontal manner will create a movement on the film that you did not plan and probably do not want. Unintentional movements, for either the camera or the subject, can be very distracting, and may totally ruin the effect you want to create.

In choosing a tripod for animation you must look for the sturdiest model. It should extend at least four feet from the floor and still remain steady. When shooting, it is wise to stand back from the tripod, using the single-framing cable release provided with most cameras. Watch out for people who might walk through the room shaking the tripod as they go, or pets who might disrupt the whole shooting.

For real control of the shooting, look into an animation stand. A simple animation stand can easily be constructed (see page 156 for instructions and illustration). It is simply a solid wooden stand on which to mount the camera. It need not take up too much room or be expensive to build. Also available is an animation stand designed especially for Super-8mm cameras and made by Oxberry, the leading manufacturer of professional animation equipment. The Oxberry Animator 8 is the best 8mm animation system available. It is a complete system, and comes with a Super-8mm camera with zoom lens and camera mount. You can photograph single frame, live action, and time lapse with dissolves, fades, and multiple exposures. The kit includes two flood lamps, a no-glare glass platen, and a background cell. The cost of the stand is about $600, but it offers possibilities for all kinds of animation, including paper animation, cutout animation, puppet animation, and cell animation. It can be adjusted to photograph in either a vertical or horizontal position.

A stand is excellent for many kinds of animation, particularly the animation of cutouts or artwork, subjects in two dimensions. But there is no need to feel limited by the lack of an animation stand, for much two-dimensional animation can be done with your camera on a tripod. The results may not look as professional as they would if done on a stand, but with care they can be just as effective. Paper cutouts can be made and attached to a background hanging on a wall. The camera can then be lined up with the lens horizontal to the wall and you can move the cutouts in any pattern you wish.

Lighting should be very simple. You need only two lights, one on each side of the camera. Work with the lights to reduce shadows and glares, and keep this in mind when selecting materials to be photographed. It is not a good idea to use shiny paper or other objects that might produce glares and reflections from the lights.

When you have gathered all the necessary equipment, you are ready to plan your animation. Suppose you begin with a stuffed animal, and you want it to move across a background from left to right in the frame. First you must decide on a background. It can be as simple as a piece of plain construction paper, but it should not be shiny. You might want to draw or paint a background of trees, a garden, or a row of houses.

Once the background is complete, you must decide on the movement you want the animal to make. Lightly mark the point on the background where the edge of the frame comes. Then look through the camera and have a friend move the animal in and out of the frame. Mark the points on the background at which the animal will appear and at which it will stop or disappear. Measure the distance between the points, and with a light pencil draw a series of dots charting the path along which the animal will move.

After you have measured the distance to be traveled, you must decide how much screen time the movement is to take. If you are planning to project and to shoot the film at eighteen frames per second, and you decide that the movement should take five seconds, you can figure the screen time by multiplying 5 times 18—ninety frames for the move. To figure out how much the animal will move on each frame, measure the total distance to be traveled and divide it by the total number of frames to be used. The result will tell you how far to move the animal for each exposure. If you want the animal to pause, shoot several frames of it in the same position, then continue the move.

There are three things to remember: First, once the first frame is exposed, the camera must not change position horizontally until the shot is complete. Second, once the first frame is exposed, the background must not change position until the shot is complete. Third, once the first frame is exposed, do not move anything in the frame except the piece or pieces for which the movement is planned until the shot is complete.

You can change the field size of the camera at any time either by using your zoom lens or by changing lenses or by moving the camera toward or away from the subject (but it is not wise to move the camera unless you are using an animation stand). In animation, just as in live action, you will want to use close-ups, medium shots, and long shots, but in animation everything must be planned before the first frame is shot.

Once you have a basic understanding of how animation

works, you are free to animate anything your imagination can produce. One of the most popular kinds is cutout animation. You can write a story, cut out paper figures, hinge the figures at the joints with paper fasteners, and animate arms, legs, tails, ears, heads, even fingers. You can do the same with pictures from a magazine or a storybook.

Clay figures are easy to animate. Use modeling clay. Color it, if you like, with food coloring. You can animate a ball of clay growing into a figure. Start by shooting several seconds of the ball of clay. Do not move the camera. Pull the clay into two balls. Shoot several more seconds. Make a flat, round head. Shoot several frames. Attach a body to the head. Shoot several more frames. Add arms and legs. A few more frames. Add a hat, and make the figure wave at the camera. When you project your finished film it will look as if your figure grew by itself from a ball of clay.

You can use many kinds of art materials for animation. Try making a ball of string unravel, then wind up again by itself. Make a collage of tissue paper, then animate the collage by having each piece of tissue wiggle. Use very few frames for each shot of a moving piece of tissue, and when you are finished the whole collage will seem to come to life.

Perhaps the most fun of animation comes from animating real objects and people. For instance, you can make a chair fall over and then pick itself up—all by itself. Try making shoes walk across the floor, with nobody wearing them. Take a room in your house, say the kitchen. You can make the refrigerator open, the milk jump to the counter, the cupboard open, a glass come out, and the milk pour itself into the glass. You can make tricycles roll down the street by themselves and turn the corner. Have a friend sit on the ground as if he were driving a car. Then move him out of the driveway, into the street, and down to the corner. Make him go forward and backward. When your film is done, your friend will appear to be driving down the street by the seat of his pants.

You can animate anything you can move. There is no end to the possibilities. Give your mind free rein and see where your imagination leads you.

APPENDIX:

Building an Animation Stand

You can build your own inexpensive animation stand with materials found at any good lumberyard and hardware store. The base of your stand should be a three-foot-square piece of plywood, finished on one side. Paint it black to avoid unwanted reflections into the camera lens. To mount the camera you will need three 3-foot pieces of slotted angle iron—the kind used for making adjustable shelves. Attach two of them on either side of the black baseboard for vertical supports. Attach the third between the two verticals to provide a support for the camera. Mount the verticals to the baseboard with short pieces of angle iron. Mount the horizontal between the verticals with short bolts and wing nuts. Center the camera on the horizontal bar and mount it with a short ¼-inch machine screw. Since the mounting socket on your camera is not very deep, you may need some washers on the ¼-inch screw to make the camera fit perfectly tight.

To vary the field size, you can raise or lower the horizontal bar. To help ensure a constant field size, attach a yardstick to one of the verticals for a quick reference when changing camera heights for different shots. Mount two lights on opposite sides of the vertical supports. Artwork can be held flat during photography with a twelve-inch-square piece of Tru-site glass, available from any picture-framing

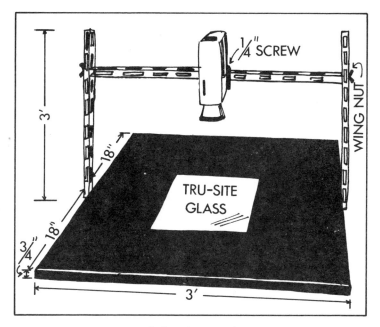

Animation stand

shop. Cover the edges with masking tape to protect yourself from cuts. The textured surface should be placed toward the camera lens.

Index

SCOT
EILSTON